P9-EMG-930

DATE DUE

OCT 19 '98			
NOV 2 '98			
NOV 24 '98			
DEC 22 '98			
JAN 24 '99			
FEB 9 '99			
JUN 15 '99			
20 '99			
NOV 2 '99			
SEP 24 00			
NOV 26 '99			
JAN 16 04			
JUL 15 04			
MAR 9 07			
NOV 4 12			

DEMCO 38-297

Dinosaurs
by Design

Dinosaurs by Design

Duane T. Gish, Ph.D.

Edited by
Gloria Clanin

Illustrated by
Earl & Bonita Snellenberger

MB
Master Books

About the Author

Dr. Duane Gish is a man who, in addition to his accomplishments as a speaker and writer, is known by many as the foremost creationist debater in the world today. His travels have taken him to virtually every state in the continental U.S. and into 30 countries. Dr. Gish is listed in American Men of Science and Who's Who in the West. He is a member of the American Chemical Society, the American Association for the Advancement of Science, and is a Fellow of the American Institute of Chemists.

Dr. Gish received his Ph.D. in biochemistry in 1953 from the University of California, Berkeley. His interest in the creation/evolution issue grew until, in 1971, he left The Upjohn Company to join the faculty at the newly established (1970) Christian Heritage College and its research division. In 1972, the latter changed its name to the Institute for Creation Research, and Dr. Gish has served as Associate Director and Vice President since that time.

Dedication

This book is dedicated to Masami Usami, M.D., of Mito, Japan, President of the Creation Science Association of Japan, for his dedicated, selfless, and untiring efforts to make known the truth of God's creation to the people of Japan.

Acknowledgement

The author wishes to acknowledge that this book is the product of a major team effort. The artwork gives obvious testimony to the artistic abilities of the artists, Earl and Bonnie Snellenberger, but their work also involved many hours of researching each subject. Special thanks are due to the production manager, Gloria Clanin, who designed this book, and put in countless hours, not only as production manager, but also in research, editing, and other areas. Thanks are also due to Barrie Lyons for research and editing, to John Rajca, whose technical assistance and overview of the subject has been invaluable, and to Ron Hight, for production assistance and final layout.

First printing: 1992
Sixth printing: April 1996

ISBN: 0-89051-165-9
Library of Congress Number: 93-144873

Scriptures quoted from the
New King James Version

Printed in China

Table of Contents

The World of Dinosaurs

Parasaurolophus

Struthiomimus

Baryony

Maiasaura

Ultrasaurus

Styracosaurus

Saltasaurus

Ankylosaurids

Spinosaurus

Iguanodon

Plateosaurus

Velociraptor

Psittacosaurus

Tsintaosaurus

Leaellynosaura

Allosaurus

Compsognathus

Kentrosaurus

7

How Fossils Are Formed

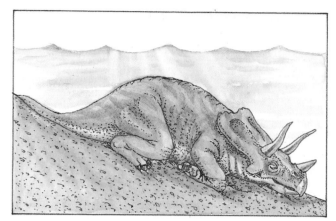

1

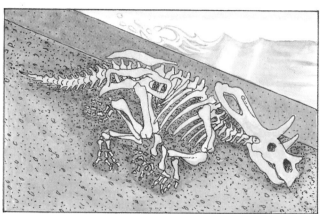

2

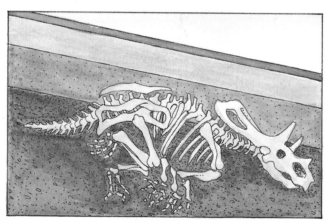

3

4

A fossil is a part of an animal or a plant that has been dead a long time—usually thousands of years. In order for a plant or an animal to become a fossil (except under very special circumstances), it must be buried almost immediately after it dies. If an animal dies, and then just lies around on the ground or floats around in the water, it never becomes a fossil.

First of all, dead plants and animals—especially animals—decompose very quickly due to bacteria and natural chemical processes. Second, there are a lot of insects, worms, and animals (called scavengers) that eat dead things. Third, oxidation by oxygen in the air causes animals and plants to decompose. Finally, there are chemicals in water and the ground—such as acids—which decompose and dissolve everything, including bones and teeth.

What happens to a bone, a tooth, or a plant when it becomes a fossil? What usually happens is everything in the bone or plant is replaced, a tiny bit at a time, by minerals dissolved in the water that is in the ground. As water moves through the ground, it carries various kinds of minerals—such as silica (silicon dioxide [SiO_2]), calcite (calcium carbonate [$CaCO_3$]), and pyrite (iron disulfide, [FeS_2])—along with it. When the bones and teeth of an animal, or parts of a plant buried in the ground, become wet with this water, the mineral in the water replaces all the material in the bone, tooth, or plant, and it

1. All dinosaurs not on Noah's Ark were drowned in the Flood.
2. Animal was buried rapidly as the Flood deposited soft layers of material that later turned to stone.
3. Fossilization occured as the animal lay buried deeply beneath Flood sediment.
4. Fossils become exposed as the ground around animal erodes away.

becomes hard as a rock. In fact, it is now a rock, but it has almost the exact shape of the bone, tooth, or plant it replaces. It doesn't take millions or even thousands of years for something to become a fossil.

Someone found, down in an old abandoned mine shaft, a hat that a miner had lost 50 years earlier. The hat was as hard as rock. After lying at the bottom of the shaft in water with a lot of mineral, the hat had fossilized. The miner's soft hat was now a hard hat!

Once in awhile, very rarely, an animal is frozen quickly and stays frozen for several thousand years. For example, a few mammoths (huge woolly elephants) in Alaska and Siberia were somehow frozen very quickly thousands of years ago and have been found recently with their flesh still good enough to eat. The fossil bones of thousands of animals have been taken out of the La Brea tar pits in Los Angeles, California. The tar didn't keep the flesh of these animals from rotting away, but it did prevent the bones from decomposing or disappearing.

Fossil studies give us evidence of a worldwide catastrophe, such as a flood. We have already mentioned that a fossil is formed when a plant or animal is buried very quickly after it dies. If there is time for it to rot or decompose slowly, it will not retain its form or composition. A flood would cause sudden burial and provide a natural means of fossilizing their bones.

Fossils of dinosaurs and many other animals have been found in all parts of the world; many have been dug up in places where they could not survive the climate that exists there today. How could they have existed there? Apparently a drastic change in climate has occurred since that time.

Scientists agree that there was a drastic change of climate at one time in the earth's history, but they have many different reasons for it. Creationists believe that the Flood changed the earth's climate.

Dinosaur National Monument, Utah

Fossils of dinosaurs have been found in just about every place in the world, from Alaska and Siberia to Antarctica. Many have been found in Canada, the U.S. (especially in some of the western states such as Colorado, Utah, Montana, and Wyoming), China, Mongolia, Europe, Africa, Mexico, South America, and Australia. Sometimes the fossils of many dinosaurs are found all jumbled together in a huge fossil graveyard, just as you would expect if they had been tossed around in a gigantic flood.

All we have left today to tell us about the creatures that roamed the entire earth long ago are the many fossil bones, fossil footprints, and fossil eggs. But finding them in areas where no dinosaurs could live today provides further evidence of the Flood as recorded in the Bible.

Digging Up Dinosaur Fossils

When you think of buried treasure do you picture a pirate's chest or prospecting for gold? Well, looking for fossils is also hunting for buried treasure.

Paleontologists and amateurs scour the world looking for new "treasures." The word "amateur" doesn't really apply here. It takes a great deal of time and practice to get your "eye in" (that means that you can recognize a fossil when you see it). This is not nearly as easy as you might think. Often the first thing searchers see may only be a small fossil bone or bone fragment sticking out of an eroded hillside or sea cliff. Who knows, perhaps that small bone is the tip of a *Triceratops'* tail, or the edge a great field of fossils.

When we think of fossils, we usually think of fossilized bones, but there are five kinds of animal fossils. The other types are: footprints, coprolites (animal droppings), skin impressions, and dinosaur eggs. Each of these plays a part in learning more about dinosaurs and how they lived.

Sometimes discoveries are made by accident as new roads are built, railroad beds cut out of mountains, mines dug, or perhaps by a farmer plowing a new field.

Locating fossils is only the beginning. Freeing a large dinosaur from the rock in which it's buried is a job for a team of experts. We think of large dinosaur bones as being heavy and durable. They were when the dinosaur was alive, but they're not bones anymore, they're fossils. Fossils need careful handling because they are fragile and can easily be destroyed.

Surprisingly, one of first things the "experts" may do is bring in bulldozers to move tons of rock. If great amounts of rock need to be moved, to uncover the fossils, they may even use dynamite. As the workers get closer to the brittle fossils, the work gets more careful. Picks and shovels may be utilized in the next step.

As soon as the bones are uncovered—but still in the ground—the mapping begins. This step is *very* important. An exact diagram of the fossil location is made. Each fossil is

numbered, measured, photographed, and notes are made.

All of this is vital for the people who will be assembling the dinosaur. The fossils may wait in a museum or warehouse for years until assembly can begin. If the information about the fossils isn't accurate and complete, it may be nearly impossible to put the dinosaur together correctly.

As work progresses on the dinosaur "dig," hand tools such as chisels, hammers, brushes, toothbrushes, etc. are used. A needle may be used to remove individual grains of sand. In the Sahara Desert, you can simply brush the sand away from the fossil. Protective goggles may be worn to protect the workers' eyes, and hard hats are necessary near cliffs.

At times, the bones are so small and delicate that they are left in a block of rock to be separated in the museum laboratory under more controlled conditions.

Once a fossil is exposed to the air and humidity, it will begin to deteriorate. To harden the fossil, it may be sprayed with resin, or painted with glue or shellac. Pieces that break are carefully glued back together.

Large bones present special problems, and must be handled very carefully. Their weight makes them susceptible to breaking and crumbling. First, a little more that half of the bone is freed from the rock. Next, wet tissue paper is spread over the exposed surface to protect it. Then, sackcloth bandages soaked in plaster of paris are used to cover the surface. When this has hardened, the rest of the fossil is freed and carefully turned over. The procedure is then repeated on the second side. When the plaster jacket has hardened, it is ready to be transported.

Preparing the preserved fossils for the trip to the museum can be quite a job. The larger fossils, in their plaster jackets, may need to be lifted into a truck with a crane. Smaller fossils will be packed in crates. Again, careful note-taking is done. All the fossils must be accounted for, and the crates labeled.

Having been carefully prepared, these "treasures" are loaded on trucks for their often bumpy ride or flight to a museum.

OTHER KINDS OF FOSSIL REMAINS

Footprints

Coprolites

Skin Impressions

Eggs and Nests

Restoring Dinosaur Fossils

The task of rebuilding a dinosaur from the crates of fossils to finished reconstruction can take five years or more.

The job of identifying the dinosaur to which the fossils belong is often very difficult. When we see a reconstructed skeleton in a museum or a photograph in a book, it's pretty obvious what kind of dinosaur it is. Since it is very rare for a complete dinosaur skeleton to be found, a lot of educated guesses must be made. Not only are pieces of the skeleton missing, but fossils of several types of dinosaurs can be mixed together in large fossil graveyards. This would be like putting together a huge jigsaw puzzle. You not only don't have the picture on the cover to guide you, but not all of the pieces are there and pieces of many puzzles may be mixed together!

Once the dinosaur has been identified, missing bones can be molded from plaster or glass-fiber substitutes. A missing left hip bone may be molded from the right hip bone that was found. Museums may even make a cast of a fossil to share with another museum that needs it. If all else fails, a fossil from a similar type of dinosaur may be used.

The laboratory technicians who free the fossils from rock and repair broken fossils are called preparators. In the field, the fossils were "cleaned" so they could be transported. Now the preparators will remove every trace of rock. This is very delicate work. If they damage or mark the fossil in any way, mistakes could be made when the fossil is assembled.

By studying the fossils, scientists can tell how a dinosaur was built, if it stood on two feet, or walked on all fours. They may be able to tell how the animal carried its body as it walked or ran. The braincase, eye sockets, teeth, backbone, muscle scars, and bony ridges that anchored muscles all tell something important about the animal. If a fossil is scratched, repaired incorrectly, or improperly prepared, important clues can be missed or misinterpreted.

To clean the fossils of unwanted rock and their protective jackets, many different methods are practiced. A full range of tools is used: from pneumatic chisels, sandblasting with tiny jets of gas and fine abrasive powder, down to high-powered microscopes for cleaning the most delicate areas. Dental tools are aften used, including high-speed drills with diamond cutting wheels, similar to the ones your dentist may have used on you. A wonderful little tool is the vibropen, whose fast-vibrating tip seems to eat away at the rock encasing the fossil as if it were butter.

Under certain conditions a fossil can be given an acid bath. If the preparator feels the acid bath won't harm the fossil itself, it will be soaked in a container of dilute acid. Different acids are used depending on the type of rock the fossil is embedded in.

Using modern tools, the preparators can "see" inside unhatched fossil eggs. X-rays and CAT (computerized axial tomography) scans are used to examine the delicate fossils and give valuable information.

Once all the fossils are cleaned, reproduced, and accounted for, the next phase begins. Assembling the prepared fossils into a standing dinosaur can be a minor engineering feat. Two of the first problems that need to be

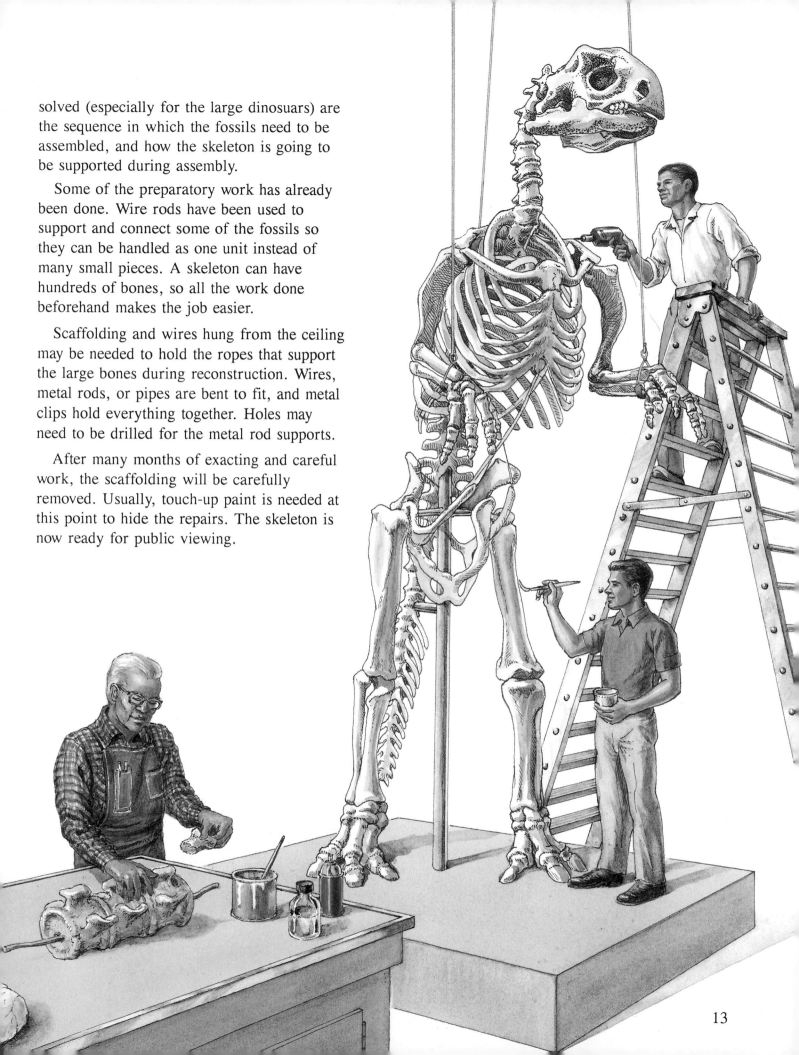

solved (especially for the large dinosaurs) are the sequence in which the fossils need to be assembled, and how the skeleton is going to be supported during assembly.

Some of the preparatory work has already been done. Wire rods have been used to support and connect some of the fossils so they can be handled as one unit instead of many small pieces. A skeleton can have hundreds of bones, so all the work done beforehand makes the job easier.

Scaffolding and wires hung from the ceiling may be needed to hold the ropes that support the large bones during reconstruction. Wires, metal rods, or pipes are bent to fit, and metal clips hold everything together. Holes may need to be drilled for the metal rod supports.

After many months of exacting and careful work, the scaffolding will be carefully removed. Usually, touch-up paint is needed at this point to hide the repairs. The skeleton is now ready for public viewing.

How Long Ago Did Dinosaurs Live?

Above us are two men visiting the Grand Canyon in Arizona for the first time. Each man is looking at the canyon and drawing conclusions as to how it may have been formed, based on whether he believes in creation or evolution. That means each man is drawing conclusions based on his bias or preconceived ideas.

For scientists to be able to say something has been proven, it has to be observable and it has to be repeatable. If it's not, then it's considered a hypothesis (educated guess).

Evolutionists have suggested several theories of how the Grand Canyon was formed. One of the more popular theories was that the Grand Canyon was cut by the Colorado River. Today, however, geologists who are knowledgeable about the Grand Canyon are less inclined to believe that theory.

Geologist Dr. Steve Austin has spent years studying the Grand Canyon. He has found evidence in support of the theory that the canyon was formed by the breaking of great natural dams that had held back enormous lakes. Creationists believe waters, trapped by these dams soon after Noah's Flood, eroded the Grand Canyon. Their waters cut through sedimentary layers believed to have been laid down by the Flood.

If these ancient lakes did exist, they would have covered a large portion of the "Colorado Plateau" (high flatland areas of Utah, Colorado, Arizona, and New Mexico). The lakes could easily have covered an area of more than 30,000 square miles, and contained 3,000 cubic miles of water.

Scientists know that a hurricane, normal flood, or tidal wave can do more in an hour or a day than the ordinary processes of nature can do in a thousand years. Can you imagine what the flood waters of these immense lakes would do?

When we try to estimate how long ago dinosaurs lived, we have only the evidence that exists today. We have to take the dinosaur fossils, look at all the evidence we can find about them, and draw conclusions based on as many facts as possible.

One piece of evidence is the rocks in which we find dinosaur fossils. The question is—how old are the rocks? According to the theory of evolution, the rocks can be many millions of years old. When you find a dinosaur bone, it is not at all obvious how old it is. In fact, it is very difficult to even guess. When an evolutionist claims that a particular fossil's age is hundreds of millions of years, he bases this guess on the age of the rock in which it is found. The rock's age, in turn, is estimated by comparing it with similar rocks that have been dated using radioactive methods. There is good reason for scientists to be skeptical of those radioactive methods, for they often give very unreliable results.

Evolutionists also believe that the age of a rock can be determined by the *presumed* age of the fossil found in it. This is called circular reasoning. It is also assumed that it may have taken millions of years for some of the strata (layers of sedimentary rock) to be laid down.

Uniformitarianism is the belief

that the present is the key to the past, and that geologic processes have usually proceeded at the same rate they do today. Local floods, volcanic action, and other similar events, they believe, are enough to explain the earth as it is today.

Creationists, however, believe a better explanation for the earth's geology is *catastrophism*—geologic changes made during rapid and catastrophic events. These changes would probably have had long periods of slow and gradual change between them.

Noah's Flood was certainly an event of catastrophic proportions! A worldwide Flood and the events during it would have changed the face of the earth in ways that we should be able to see today.

Dr. Austin believes that, looking at all the evidence, "It is reasonable to think that fossils and rocks could have formed rapidly only thousands of years ago."

We may not have all the answers yet, but I have never found anything to make me doubt the truth of God's Word, the Bible.

Are there dinosaurs living today? That's an intriguing question, and you can count on it to start a lively conversation any time this question is discussed.

If the dinosaurs really did live 70 to 225 million years ago as evolutionists suggest, it would be pretty hard to suppose that dinosaurs still exist today. But, if the earth were just a few thousand years old and two of each kind of land animal survived on Noah's Ark, then it is possible a few could still be surviving today.

On April 26, 1890, an article appeared in the *Tombstone Epitaph* that amazed even the most skeptical reader.

According to the story, two men were riding in the desert outside Tombstone, Arizona when they looked up and saw an enormous flying creature gliding through the air, feet extended, preparing to land. The horses and men were frantic with fear.

Could this be the Thunderbird of Indian legend? American Indian tribes from Alaska to Mexico had legends of a gigantic flying monster. All the legends had in common the huge size and power of this creature. Thunder was said to be the noise of its wings in flight, and Indians believed as it flew through the clouds it ripped them open bringing the rain.

When these cowboys got a closer look at this flying creature on the ground they were amazed. Besides having huge wings, it had a long, slim body with great claws on its feet and on the front of its wings. They said its eight-foot-long head was similar to an alligator, with a mouth full of teeth, but had large protruding eyes.

The men, it was said, killed it and cut off its wing tip for a trophy. The creature's wing was a smooth, tough membrane—like a bat's.

Was this fantastic tale true or just an imaginary tale of a small town newspaper reporter after visiting one too many saloons? I think most people would assume this was just a flight of fancy. The description fits the Pteranodon family of flying reptiles rather closely, however. It especially fits the description of the *Quetzalcoatlus* fossil found in Texas in 1972.

Those two cowboys may have shot the last living *Quetzalcoatlus* just a little over 100 years ago. It is an unlikely story, but who knows?

Everyone has heard about the Loch Ness Monster, affectionately known as Nessie. And everyone has an opinion as to whether Nessie really exists or not.

Loch Ness is a long (24½ miles), cold (42° F.), very deep (over 900 feet) lake in northern Scotland. This lake, as are many others, is connected to the sea by waterways.

Some scientists believe Nessie and relatives travel between the North Sea and Lake Ness on the River Ness, to feed on migratory fish.

One of the reasons it's so hard to see anything in the lake is that the lake is filled with very fine particles of peat suspended in the water.

Serious scientific investigation finally began in October of 1970 when a group of scientists probed Loch Ness with high-frequency sonar. "Something massive" passed through the sonar beam, and 10 minutes later "similar but larger objects were detected from greater distances." Two years later an even more ambitious investigation began and had similar results. *Something* is down there, but what? In 1975 an incredible (but fuzzy) underwater photograph was taken of what some believe to be Nessie. Based on this photo, above-water sightings, and other photos, some people believe Nessie to be an *Elasmosaurus*.

Is planet Earth fully explored? Not quite. Even in the day of satellite photos there are still many areas about which we know little. In the Ndoki (*en-DOE-key*) region of northern Congo there is an area into which man has seldom, if ever, ventured. It is seven and one-half million acres of dense jungle and treacherous swamp into which even the adventurous pygmies have seldom ventured.

This is the home of the animal the pygmies call Mokele Mbembe (*mo-KEE-le MEM-be*). They have described it as brownish-gray, smooth skinned, much larger than an elephant, with a "very long tail, as powerful as a crocodile's."

When shown pictures of many different animals, they picked *Apatasaurus*-like animals as looking the most like Mokele Mbembe.

A few expeditions have braved the jungle and swamps to try and find proof that there really is such a creature living. They can stay in the jungle only a short time, due to limited visas, weather, tsetse flies, and other difficulties.

If these dinosaur-like animals do exist, I hope they find one, before the last of these animals has perished.

Dinosaur Family Life

We can observe animals living today and know what they like to eat, how they reproduce, and whether they live in holes in the ground or nests high in treetops. It is much harder to discover these same facts if there are no living specimens to watch.

When dinosaur fossils were first found, many ideas were suggested concerning their nature. Few facts were known, so one idea seemed as good as the next. In 1922, a great discovery was made. In the Flaming Cliffs area of the Gobi Desert (Mongolia), dinosaur eggs were found.

They were the eggs of a fairly small (6-foot-long) dinosaur called *Protoceratops* (PRO-toe-SAIR-ah-tops). Finally, scientists knew that at least some dinosaurs laid eggs. The mother *Protoceratops* laid her eggs in a nest that was little more than a hollow in the ground. The 8-inch-long eggs were almost sausage-shaped, and, in a circle pointing outwards.

Over 30 eggs were found in each of several nests. It may be that several females shared the same nest. The young dinosaurs must have stayed pretty close to home as they were growing up, because fossils of all sizes—from newly hatched to adult—were found near the nesting sites.

We may have fossil evidence of a parent protecting its young. Fossil remains were found of an adult *Protoceratops* locked in deadly combat with a meat-eating *Velociraptor*.

In 1978, in Montana, a very special discovery was made. A dinosaur's nest was found that not only had fossil eggs in it, but also the bones of fossilized babies. They were over three feet long and 12 inches high. It is believed they were about a month old.

The dinosaur that laid these eggs was given the name *Maiasaura* (MY-ah-SORE-ah) which means "good mother lizard." They were large (up to 30 feet long), plant-eating, duck-billed dinosaurs.

The *Maiasaura* raised their babies in nurseries. The nests were close together (23 feet apart) so the parents could help each other guard the babies from predators.

These were not small nests like chickens make. They were mounds of dirt 6–7 feet across. The mother *Maiasaura* would push dirt into a pile and then scrape out a 3-foot-deep bowl shape in the middle. None of her eggs could accidentally roll out of a nest that deep!

It is believed she would cover the nest with vegetation and let the sun and rotting plants warm the eggs. Today, crocodiles incubate their eggs in the same way. The mother *Maiasaura* most likely sat next to her nest to protect her babies from predators and from accidentally being stepped on by other dinosaurs.

When the babies hatched, it is believed they were not sufficiently developed to leave the nest and hunt for their own food. The mother *Maiasaura* brought food to her little ones (illustration) until they were a year or two old.

The hatchling *Maiasauras* grew so fast—from about 16 inches to 58 inches in only a year—some scientists believe they *may* have been warm-blooded animals.

As more studies are done, ideas and theories about dinosaurs are changing. Everyone used to believe all dinosaurs were cold-blooded and sluggish, especially when the temperature was cold. Now, as scientists study dinosaurs' anatomy more closely, they find some similarities between dinosaurs and modern mammals.

It is now thought by some that they may have hunted in packs, lived in colonies, and were sleeker, faster, and more maneuverable than previously believed. Trying to imagine behavior based on fossils, however, is difficult and questionable.

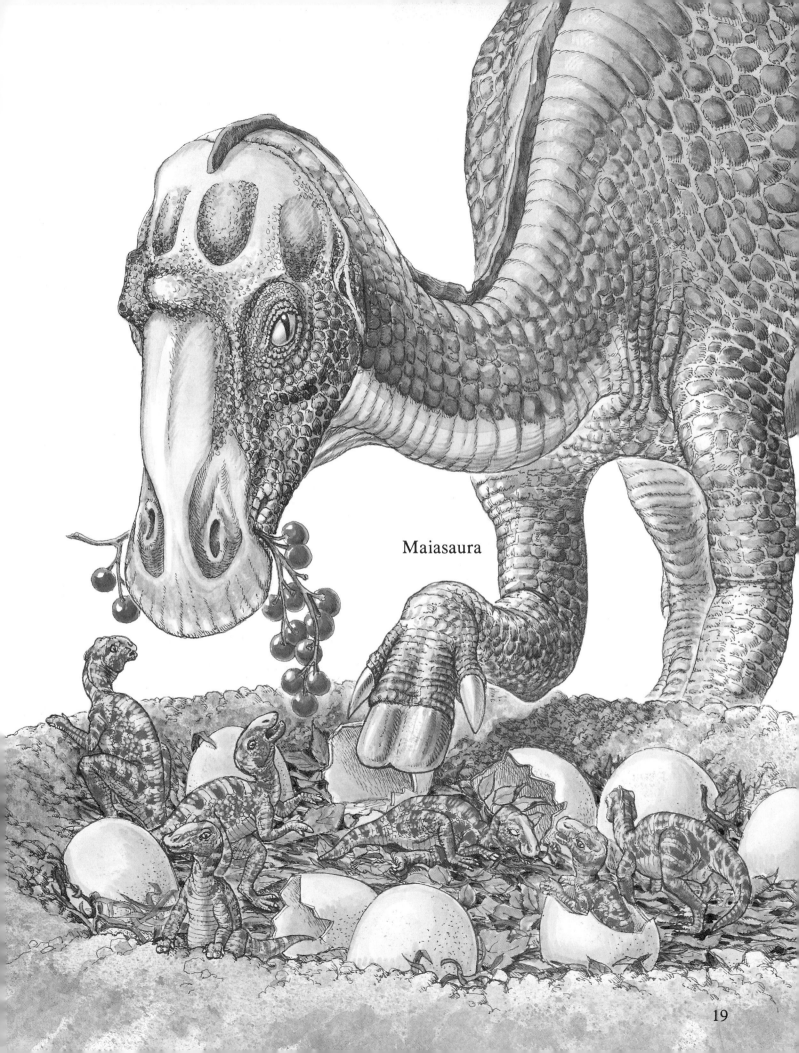

Maiasaura

Are There Dinosaurs in the Bible?

We know that God created dinosaurs because God created all living things. God created man and dinosaurs on the sixth day of creation.

> Then God said, "Let the earth bring forth the living creature according to its kind: cattle and creeping thing and beast of the earth, each according to its kind"; and it was so.
>
> And God made the beast of the earth according to its kind, cattle according to its kind, and everything that creeps on the earth according to its kind. And God saw that it was good.
>
> Then God said, "Let Us make man in Our image, according to Our likeness; let them have dominion over the fish of the sea, over the birds of the air, and over the cattle, over all the earth and over every creeping thing that creeps on the earth."

Genesis 1:24-26

If God created dinosaurs along with all the other animals (and Adam and Eve), then why don't we find the word "dinosaur" anywhere in the Bible? The answer is simple. The Bible was translated into English in about 1600, but fossils of dinosaurs were not discovered until almost 250 years later and the word "dinosaur" didn't exist until 1840.

Even though the Bible doesn't use the word "dinosaur," the Bible does describe an animal that must have been a dinosaur. This is found in Job, Chapter 40.

> "Look now at the behemoth, which I made along with you; He eats grass like an ox.
>
> See now, his strength is in his hips, and his power is in his stomach muscles.
>
> He moves his tail like a cedar; the sinews of his thighs are tightly knit.

> His bones are like beams of bronze, his ribs like bars of iron.
>
> He is the first of the ways of God; only He who made him can bring near His sword.
>
> Surely the mountains yield food for him, and all the beasts of the field play there.
>
> He lies under the lotus trees, in a covert of reeds and marsh.
>
> The lotus trees cover him with their shade; the willows by the brook surround him.
>
> Indeed the river may rage, yet he is confident, though the Jordan gushes into his mouth.
>
> Though he takes it in his eyes, or one pierces his nose with a snare."

Job 40:15-24

Some people have suggested that this creature that the Bible calls a behemoth was an elephant. But have you ever seen the tail of an elephant? The tail of an elephant certainly doesn't look like a cedar tree, does it? Besides, the behemoth was so big he thought he could drink up a river, even the Jordan river, and wouldn't even have to be in a hurry to do it! Have you ever seen an elephant that big? There is no animal on the earth today that even comes close to being as big and fearsome as the behemoth described in the Bible. But, as we will see, the description of the behemoth sounds very much like what we would expect of an *Apatosaurus*, or perhaps the huge *Brachiosaurus*, or some other great big dinosaur.

Thus, the Bible gives us information that humans and dinosaurs really did live at the same time, a long time ago, for here in the Book of Job we find a good description of a dinosaur. This tells us that people in those ancient times, after the great Flood of Noah, still remembered dinosaurs.

Job tells us about another great animal—called leviathan—that lived in water.

Job 41—all 34 verses—describes a very fearsome beast. These verses tell of an animal that can't be caught, is very hard to kill, and if you do battle with him, you won't want to try it again. The very sight of him causes so much fear that people cringe in fright. Leviathan has no fear of man nor other animals. He is discussed again on pages 82 and 83.

When did this man (Job) live? Since he is describing dinosaurs, it would be most helpful to put him in a time period.

We are not given an exact date for Job, but we do have several clues. It is believed that Job is the oldest book in the Bible except for the first 11 chapters of Genesis.

He certainly lived before the days of Moses, since there is no mention of the Ten Commandments or the Mosaic laws. As a humble servant of God, if he had known the laws of God, he would have quoted them often. But, the Bible says that he "was blameless and upright, and one who feared (honored) God and shunned evil" (Job 1:1). God's laws were known to men and women from the very beginning.

Most scholars place Job around 2,000 B.C., after the Flood of Noah, but before great cities were built.

The animals described in the book of Job were alive after the Flood. No dinosaurs, as far as has been determined, still survive today. The leviathan, possibly the dragon of widespread legends, certainly has not survived to this day. From our reading of the record in the Bible and our study of fossils we have very good evidence concerning the nature, structure, and way of life of these very unusual and fascinating creatures.

Early Fossil Discoveries

Iguanodon tooth

The Tooth that Started it All

Dr. Gideon Mantell was an English doctor who lived near Oxford, England, and liked to collect fossils. His wife, Mary, shared his interest in fossils, and they often went out looking for them.

One day in the spring of 1822, Mary rode along in the carriage with him when he went to call on a patient. While her husband was with his patient, she went for a walk. She noticed what appeared to be a big tooth. She showed it to her husband as soon as he came out. He had never seen anything like this before.

Dr. Mantell went to look for more fossils where his wife had found the tooth. He found not only more teeth but also several fossil bones. He realized that these were different from anything he had seen before. He turned to his wife and said, "I think you have found the remains of an animal new to science."

Since he had no idea what kind of an animal this was, he sent the bones and teeth to Baron Georges Cuvier, a famous French scientist and an expert on fossils. But this time even the expert was wrong. He thought that the teeth were from an ancient rhinoceros and the bones were from an extinct hippopotamus.

Not long after this, Dr. Mantell showed the fossil teeth to someone who was familiar with the iguana, a lizard that lives in Mexico and South America. Although the fossil teeth were much, much larger, his friend declared that they looked much like the teeth of the iguana. Dr. Mantell realized that he had found the remains of an amazing new kind of animal, a giant plant-eating, reptile-like animal. He gave it the name *Iguanodon* ("iguana tooth") (more on pages 24–25).

About this same time some fossil bones and teeth of a huge meat-eating, reptile-like animal were discovered. The creature was given the name *Megalosaurus* ("giant lizard").

Since then, the world of science has never been quite the same.

The Name "DINOSAUR"

In 1840, Sir Richard Owen, one of England's greatest anatomical researchers, closely studied the bones of *Megalosaurus* and *Iguanodon* and came to the conclusion that these were not like the bones of any animal living today. He felt they should be regarded as a new order of animal. He gave them the name "dinosaur," which means terrible lizard (*deino* = terrible; *sauros* = lizard).

The Dinosaur Wars

Although the earliest fossil finds were in Europe, great excitement was generated when new kinds of dinosaur fossils were found in western America. In 1870, two Americans, Othniel Marsh and Edward Cope, began a "dinosaur war" to see who could find the most and the best fossils.

Othniel Marsh was a wealthy man who loved fossils. He was a professor of paleontology (study of fossils) at Yale University, and used his money to help the university and to hunt for fossils.

Edward Cope was also a wealthy man. He was a genius who started taking notes on dinosaur fossils at age six. He published his first scientific paper at age 18, and at age 24 he became a professor of zoology (study of animals) at Haverford College.

These two men were friends for awhile, right after the Civil War, but soon became bitter enemies because of the desire of each to become known as the best fossil hunter in the world. They each sent teams West to locate new fossil beds. Many fossil discoveries were made by these men in Montana, Wyoming, and Colorado. The teams spied on each other, deceived each other about where they were going next, and in general carried on the "war" their bosses had started in the East.

We know a lot more today about dinosaurs than they did in 1870, but dinosaurs are just as exciting to find today as they were in the early days of dinosaur discovery.

Iguanodon

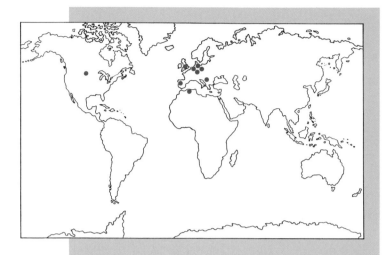

Family:
  Iguanodontidae (iguana teeth)
  Iguanodon

Fossil Locations:
  Arizona, Montana, Oklahoma, Texas, USA;
  Africa, Mongolia, Australia, Europe.

Diet:
  Plants and trees

Interesting Facts:
  • Spiked thumbs, possibly used for
    - defense against predators
    - aid in obtaining food
    - mating
  • Fossil footprints have been found in Antarctica.
  • Hard beak-shaped mouth with no teeth in
    front—chewing teeth were in back of mouth.
  • Herd of *Iguanodon* skeletons is on display at the
    Royal Institute of Natural Sciences in Belgium.

Iguanodon (*ih-GWAN-oh-DON*) has become one of the most famous dinosaurs, because he was one of the first whose fossilized parts were recognized to be a dinosaur—more than 150 years ago. You will remember that we told you about Dr. Mantell's wife (page 23) who found the tooth of a giant plant-eating, reptile-like animal that was identified as a giant lizard and later called *Iguanodon*. Dr. Mantell noted that the teeth were leaf-shaped, which confirmed the animal's diet consisted of various kinds of plants.

Until that time, no one, except very ancient people, knew that dinosaurs had ever existed. Only a few fossil bones of dinosaurs had been found, and a few fossil footprints had been seen. The very earliest finds were thought to be the bones of some big elephant or other large animal, and the three-toed footprints were thought to be those of a giant bird.

Scientists had not been able to determine exactly what *Iguanodon* and other dinosaurs really looked like because they had found only parts of the skeletons. When a sharp, beak-like bone was first found with the fossil parts of *Iguanodon*, it was supposed that it was a part of the animal's nose (round illustration). Some of the earliest scientists had thought this was some kind of large rhinoceros.

In 1877, an amazing find helped scientists discover what *Iguanodon* actually looked like. Some miners found the fossilized skeletons of more than 30 *Iguanodons* buried and piled together about 1,000 feet down in a coal mine in southwest Belgium. Many suppositions have been made as to how this huge pile of dinosaurs all met a sudden end, along with the fossilized plants that had turned into coal. It could very well have been the great Flood of Noah that caused such a catastrophe.

From the fossils found in the Belgian coal mine, scientists were able to better discern the size and distinctive parts of an *Iguanodon*. He was a big dinosaur whose strong, short front legs were probably used more like arms with hoof-like claws on the ends of his fingers.

These fossils also revealed that the cone-shaped spike (which men had formerly assumed should fit on his nose) was really a thumb on his hands! The fossilized skeletons were so complete, the entire animal could be assembled.

Because so many were found buried together, it is believed they probably lived together in herds. The fossils indicated that the females were smaller than the males.

Today, scientists know that the various species of *Iguanodon* also varied in size. The weight varied from 1½ to 5 tons. Smaller ones may have been 14 feet long, but some larger ones measure up to 33 feet in length. And they may have stood as tall as 17 feet. It is now generally agreed that they probably stood upright on their two strong hind legs and feet, but could certainly run on all four legs when they needed to.

Their mouths were formed with a toothless beak at the front, and with many ridged teeth in the cheeks. Such teeth were useful for grinding plant leaves and twigs. The large pouches inside their jaws enabled them to store food until they were ready to relax and leisurely chew their food.

Some of their footprints measure up to 20 inches in length. It is interesting, however, that there is no trace of any large tail dragging behind. *Iguanodon's* tail was apparently kept aloft and used as a counterbalance when he was walking or running. Because of his bulky size, he likely did not run fast.

The *Iguanodon* belongs to the suborder of *Ornithopods* (bird-feet), but the strong, heavy thighs that were held up by those bird feet were evidence that this was no delicate bird-like animal!

• Iguanodon

25

The Lightweights

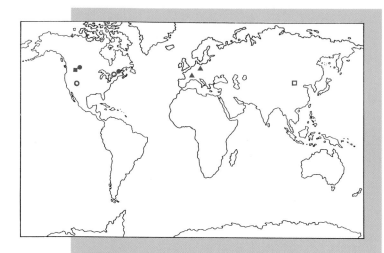

Family:
    Coelophysidae (hollow forms)
      Podokesaurus
    Compsognathidae (pretty jaws)
      Compsognathus
    Ornithomimidae (bird mimics)
      Struthiomimus
    Oviraptoridae (egg thieves)
      Oviraptor
    Troodontidae (wounding teeth)
      Troodon

Fossil Locations:
    Southwestern USA; New Jersey, USA;
    East Europe; France; Alberta, Canada;
    South Mongolia, China

Diet:
    Meat

Interesting Facts:
- Skeleton of a *Compsognathus* found in Germany had a lizard skeleton in its abdomen.
- *Struthiomimus* could probably outrun a racehorse.

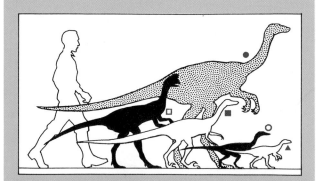

Dinosaurs of a certain group are considered lightweights, or bantamweights, because they were much smaller in size than other dinosaurs. Some of these lizard-hipped dinosaurs were as large as an ostrich; some no larger than a rooster or cat. They were all bipeds, meaning they walked on two legs.

Podokesaurus (*po-DUH-kuh-SORE-us*)—which means "swift-footed lizard"—was about 3–5 feet long and stood about 2 feet tall. Little is known about this small animal other than it belonged to the family of coelophysids that ate large insects, smaller lizards, and other smaller animals. The *Podokesaurus* had a long, flexible neck—very handy when trying to reach some lunch item in an awkward place—and a thin tail that it used as a balance when it ran.

Little **Compsognathus** (*KOMP-sog-NAY-thus*) was the smallest of the lightweight predators. Weighing about 6½ pounds, he was no bigger than a rooster or a cat. These creatures probably grubbed around for food on the ground just as chickens do today. Equipped with long, slender legs, they were able to move swiftly in pursuit of large insects or small reptiles.

Struthiomimus (*STRUTH-ee-oh-MIME-us*), means "ostrich-mimic (imitator)," since he probably looked more like an ostrich than the others (page 64). He stood 6–8 feet tall, had a small head on top of a long slender neck, and had long, thin legs that were very powerful.

He had no teeth, but *Struthiomimus* could no doubt use his beak for snapping up worms, insects, and lizards for his lunch. Unable to chew them, he probably gulped them down. He likely ate plants and fruits, also. The long claws on his powerful front legs could have been used to dig up the eggs of other dinosaurs so he could feast on the contents.

The short body and 3-foot tail of *Struthiomimus* didn't provide him with weapons, but his most valuable defenses were his powerful legs and his speed.

The **Oviraptor** (*OHV-ih-RAP-tor*), meaning "egg thief," inherited his name from the first specimen found in the Gobi Desert of Mongolia (1922). His bones were found with a nest of large dinosaur eggs; his crushed skull may have been the result of a dinosaur mother catching him in the act of stealing her eggs!

He had a large brain, but smaller head and shorter beak than the ostrich-like animals. Although his beak was toothless, he had strong jaws and two sharp spikes extending from the roof of his mouth, probably used to crush eggshells or small bones of other prey before eating them.

The word **Troodon** (*TROH-oh-don*), meaning "wounding tooth," was first assigned to an unusual tooth, but for a long time it was uncertain to which animal such teeth belonged. In 1980, more of these same teeth were discovered in Montana with remains of dinosaur nests, eggs, young and full-sized skeletons.

Probably the most outstanding feature is his teeth. They are rather flat on two sides, with curved serrated edges in front and back, and are arranged on a very thin jaw bone.

Because of his probable speed and deftness, some have called him the cheetah of the dinosaur world.

● Struthiomimus

□ Oviraptor

■ Troodon

▲ Compsognathus

○ Podokesaurus

27

Horned Dinosaurs

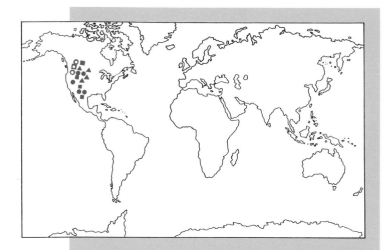

Family:

    Ceratopsidae (horned faces)

      Eucentrosaurus

      Monoclonius

      Styracosaurus

      Torosaurus

      Triceratops

Fossil Locations:

    Alberta, Canada to Mexico

Diet:

    Plants

Interesting Facts:

- Perhaps roamed in large herds.
- Probably used frills for display and defense.
- Some paleontologists have suggested they were able to run swiftly—up to 40 mph.

The family of ceratopids (*ser-ah-TOPE-ids*), or "horned faces," were the rhinoceroses of prehistoric times. These heavy-set quadrupeds had short necks and large heads and were easily identified by the horns on their faces and frills around their necks or at the back of their heads. The frills varied in size and shape, usually with a skin-covered hollow section, or "window," in the center.

Behind parrot-like beaks were sharp cheek teeth and powerful jaws fastened to the frill bone. Their bulky bodies ranged 6–30 feet long with pillar-like legs and hoof-like clawed feet.

During the early 1900s, excavations in the Canadian Red Deer River area, in northwestern United States, and as far south as Mexico, yielded hundreds of ceratopian fossils. Ceratopid remains have been found only in North America, and much is now known about them.

Triceratops (*tri-SAIR-ah-tops*) was a remarkable dinosaur with a "three-horned" face. Short frill ceratopids usually had a single long nose horn and hollow spaces, or windows, in the frill, but *Triceratops*' frill was a heavy solid bone and his nose horn was short and thick. Projecting just above his eyes were two more massive horns—up to 40 inches long—curving forward. What a menacing sight!

The first complete skull of *Triceratops* was found in 1888 on a ranch in Wyoming. It measured 7 feet long. Hundreds of bones have since been found to indicate his body was about 30 feet long, and he stood about 9½ feet tall, weighing about 6 tons—the size of a truck. Large padded feet and strong legs supported this monster.

Although he probably could charge like a rhino when being threatened, especially by *Tyrannosaurs* who may have preyed upon *Triceratops*, it is believed that he was generally

content to herd with his own kind and nibble at palm fronds with his toothless beak; then he chewed his meal heartily with the scissor-like molars in his strong jaw bones.

Eucentrosaurus (*yew-SEN-tro-SORE-us*), meaning "well-horned lizard," was called *Centrosaurus* until 1989. A large herd was found buried together in Canada. One record states that some of the bones were "broken and trampled as if they had been in a stampede . . . trying to cross a raging river"—perhaps the Great Flood of Noah?

This mid-sized ceratopid measured 20 feet long and made an awesome impression with one long spike on his nose and many small studs along the edge of his short frill. Two large spikes curved forward from the top of the frill over the hollow sections.

▲ Triceratops

Monoclonius (*MON-oh-KLONE-ee-us*) was a "one-horned" animal belonging also to the mid-size (18–20 feet long) and short frill group. His frill had only small bony knobs and was not spectacular, but the long pointed horn on his nose and his very large head—about 6 feet from the tip of his beak-shaped nose to the end of his frill—probably gave him a fearsome appearance.

Styracosaurus (*sty-RACK-oh-SORE-us*) was called the "spiked lizard" because of the long spikes that stood up on the back end of his short frill. Perhaps he flaunted his massive head when he wanted control of the herd or when he was trying to attract a mate. Because several of the horned dinosaurs are so similar, some scientists have even wondered if the more ornamental frills were the males of the same species. Despite the fancy frill, his large nose horn was probably his best weapon; it stood straight up about 2 feet high and was 6 inches thick.

A mid-sized ceratopid, he weighed 3–4 tons, stood 6 feet tall, and stretched about 18 feet long. Despite his heavy body, he had only a short, thick tail. (Because quadrupeds walked on four legs, they did not need long tails for balancing.)

Fossil findings indicate that *Styracosaurus* cared for their young until they were fully grown.

The *Torosaurus* (TORE-oh-SORE-us) was called the "bull lizard," perhaps because of his vicious looking horns. He had a short nose horn and two long eyebrow horns pointing up about 2 feet. Behind them was a very long frill with smooth edges. This frill stretched to 5½ feet wide, and his entire skull measured 8½ feet—the largest of any land animal—large enough for a small car to park on it.

Torosaurus was big. He weighed 8–9 tons and stretched about 25–26 feet from nose to tail tip. He had a massive body and short tail.

Strong Skeletons—God knew that an animal built like a Sherman tank would need special features, so He provided them with trellis-like bones in their hips for strength and to help bear the animal's weight. Both the neck and the shoulder region were also strengthened to help carry the weight of their massive heads. The first few vertebrae of the neck were welded together, and the main bones of the shoulder were also securely joined. The four toes were all strong, fairly short, and splayed out to provide a greater surface area over which to take the animal's great weight.

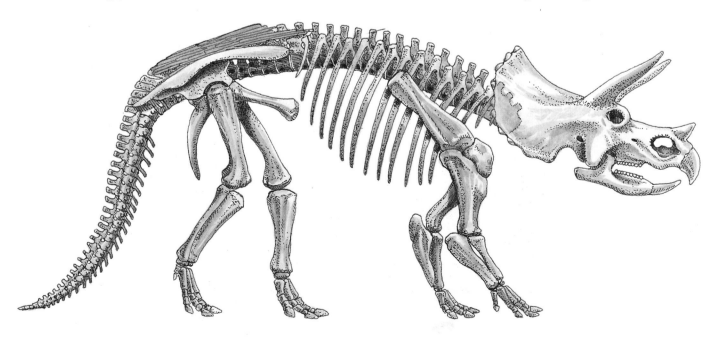

● Torosaurus

■ Monoclonius

□ Eucentrosaurus

○ Styracosaurus

31

Plated Dinosaurs

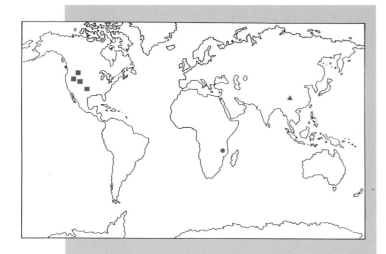

Family:

Stegosauridae (roof lizard)

Kentrosaurus

Stegosaurus

Tuojiangosaurus

Fossil Locations:

Colorado, Oklahoma, Utah, Wyoming, USA; Tanzania, East Africa; Southcentral China

Diet:

Plants

Interesting Facts:

- Had large spikes and plates on back, up to 30 inches high.
- Plates on back were perhaps heat exchangers, as they were lined with blood vessels.

The bones of a plated dinosaur were first found in North America. The large soft-boned plates on the back were then believed to lie flat to provide protection from predators; thus it was called *Stegosaurus*, a "roofed reptile." However, scientists have since found that those plates did not lie flat on the animal's back, but rather stood upward. Later, as several other types of the same dinosaur family were found in other countries, they were referred to as stegosaurs, but given their own specific name.

Certain characteristics are common to all of them. Probably the most outstanding feature of these bird-hipped dinosaurs is the plates or spines embedded in thick skin—*not on the spine*—lined up in two rows from just behind their small heads down the backs to their long tails, which were adorned with pairs of two or more spikes extending from either side.

The plates were marvels of design, sort of an early solar panel. The surface of the plate is finely grooved, suggesting that many blood vessels ran across the surface. The bony plates are honeycombed with spaces, which implies there was blood circulation to regulate body temperature.

There were many times, no doubt, when a *Stegosaurus* had to defend himself against attack by one of the meat-eating dinosaurs. In the illustration you see *Stegosaurus* whipping his spikes into an *Allosaurus*. Perhaps the *Allosaurus* finally won the battle and had the *Stegosaurus* for dinner, but you can bet he knew he had been in a fight!

Stegosaurs are only mid-sized among dinosaurs, but when full grown they were as large as 30 feet long, weighed about two tons, and stood 8–11 feet high at the hips. The back legs were nearly twice as long as the front legs, so their heads hung low near to the ground and their backs rose to full height at the hip line. The long thigh bones in the back legs were not designed for running. He probably lumbered along at a slow pace.

The heads were small and narrow for such large bodies. The mouths were like toothless beaks with small cheek teeth in back. Their small heads have caused much speculation about their intelligence, or lack of it. The size of the brain cavity in the long, narrow skull was about the size of a walnut. Whatever its capability, however, it was no doubt adequate for the needs of the stegosaurs.

A space in the tail bone was once thought to be a second brain, but it has since been decided that it was a nerve center where movements of the back legs and tail were controlled. It provided this portion of its body with quick reflex actions without waiting for the nerve signals to travel 20 feet to the brain and 20 feet back to the tail. The brain in his head did all the real thinking, of course, and had control of the voluntary movements of the rear legs and tail.

Stegosaurus (*STEG-oh-SORE-us*) was the first of these plated dinosaurs available for study, and is probably the best known. Weighing about two tons and stretching 25–30 feet from head to tail, he was also the largest of the stegosaurs.

The biggest of his sponge-like bony plates were 30 inches high and 30 inches wide. He had four 3-foot-long spikes at his tail's end. The tail was long and heavy, so he probably did not swish it around rapidly, but even moving it slowly would likely deter a rear attack.

Because his head was low when he walked on all fours, ground ferns or plants provided most of his diet. However, *Stegosaurus* could probably stand on his hind legs for a brief time to reach taller vegetation.

His brain was exceptionally small, perhaps the smallest of any dinosaur for his body size. Othniel Marsh obtained a cast of the brain cavity from a well-preserved *Stegosaurus* skull. He must have been astonished to find

■ Stegosaurus

33

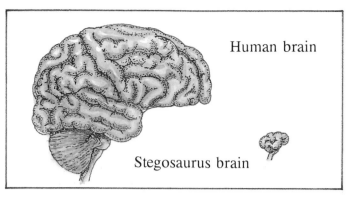

Human brain

Stegosaurus brain

Comparison of a human brain to a Stegosaurus brain

that an animal weighing up to 4,000 pounds had a brain that weighed only about 2½ ounces. Unfortunately, this led to a widely held belief that all dinosaurs were pretty stupid creatures. Later findings proved that this was not the normal situation.

Kentrosaurus (*KEN-troh-SORE-us*) was called the "spiked lizard" because of the shape of the plates on his back. He was a smaller stegosaur, usually about 8–10 feet long, although some as long as 16 feet have been reported. He was first found by a German expedition team in Tanzania, Africa, where he lived alongside the *Brachiosaurus*. Many

fossils were found and shipped back to Berlin sometime around 1912. These fossils are missing, and no one knows what happened to them. The best guess is that they were destroyed during World War II.

The plates on his back were his most unusual feature. From his neck to about midway down his back, they were triangular (and may have served as temperature modifiers), but from there to his tail they were more spiked—or cone-shaped—and stood in pairs. Another pair of spikes projected from behind his thighs. These rear spikes were likely used for self defense.

An intermediate-sized (20–23 feet long) stegosaur was *Tuojiangosaurus (toh-HWANG-o-SORE-us)*, so called for the name of the place in China where it was first found. In ancient times, Chinese thought such bones had belonged to dragons, which are prominent in Chinese history (pages 80–83).

The 15 pairs of triangular spikes on his back were smaller than those of *Stegosaurus*. He also had spikes at the end of his tail.

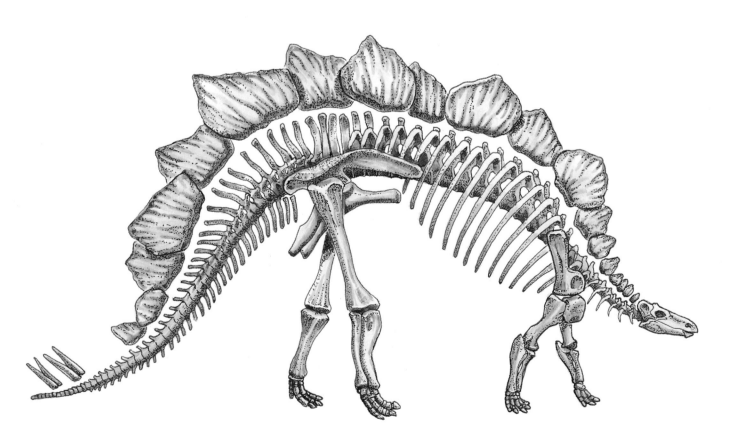

▲ Tuojiangosaurus

● Kentrosaurus

Armored Dinosaurs

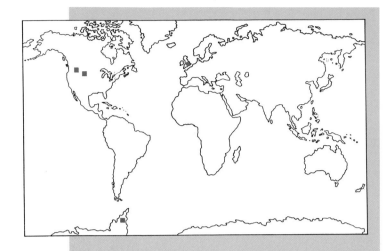

Family:
   Ankylosauridae (stiff lizards)
      Ankylosaurus
   Nodosauridae (node lizards)
      Polacanthus

Fossil Locations:
   Alberta, Canada; Montana, USA; Antarctica;
   Southeast England

Diet:
   Plants

Interesting Facts:
   • Called the armadilloes of the dinosaur world.
   • *Ankylosaurus* may have had a long flexible
     tongue for food-gathering.
   • Probably couldn't have been flipped over on
     his back if attacked.

There are several different varieties in the two major groups of armored dinosaurs, the ankylosaurids and the nodosaurids. After remains were found and reported by many people in different countries, information was overlapping. In the 1980s, the findings were all reclassified, so now we have a better understanding of which data belong to each kind. We will look at one representative from each group.

The major similarity was their appearance (the bony armor covering their backs), and the major difference was the design of the knobs and spikes in their armor.

The most recent fossil of an armored dinosaur (buried in the ice in Antarctica), was found in 1988 by an expedition to the South Pole. Although it is known to be an ankylosaurid, researchers have not yet given it a name or decided which kind it is.

The *Ankylosaurus* (*an-KILE-oh-SORE-us*) is called the "stiff lizard." He was built more like an armored tank than any other animal. He had a massive appearance: an estimated 3–5 tons in weight, 18–35 feet long, and about 4 feet tall. His skull was broad and short, helmeted with armor even over the eyelids, and had triangular horns on the back corners of his head. His short neck and barrel-shaped body were covered with the same leathery, bony knob-decorated coat of armor. The short, thick tail tapered to a rigid shaft with a large bony club at the end. It was very powerful, and that club was filled with little nodules of bone. The bones of the club are fused together making it a solid weapon for self defense. The *Daspletosaurus* (*das-PLEE-toh-SORE-us*) in the illustration looks like he just had a pretty unpleasant surprise.

The head of *Ankylosaurus* had small open passages through which he could breathe at the same time he ate (like humans do). Some believe that this may have helped to warm the air as he breathed, perhaps because his body was so shielded from the sun. His small teeth

and weak jaws indicate that his food consisted mainly of tender ground-level plants and ferns.

Polacanthus (*POL-ah-CAN-thus*), meaning "node lizard," was somewhat smaller—13 to 18 feet long and 6 feet tall—but had more dangerous looking spikes on his armor. Long projecting spines flanked either side of his bony armor, making him difficult to get near. He did not have a bony club at the end of his tail, however.

No skull has yet been found of *Polacanthus*, but a skeleton found in England was nearly complete otherwise. Not a great deal is yet known about these nodosaurids.

Daspletosaurus

● Polacanthus

■ Ankylosaurs

Duck-Billed Dinosaurs

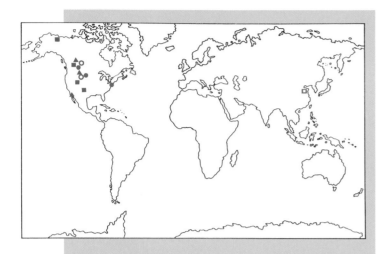

Family:

Hadrosauridae (big lizards)
Edmontosaurus
Tsintaosaurus
Lambeosauridae (Lambe's lizards)
Corythosaurus
Lambeosaurus
Parasaurolophus

Fossil Locations:

Montana, Utah, New Mexico, New Jersey, USA;
Alberta, Canada; China; Baja California, Mexico

Diet:

Plants

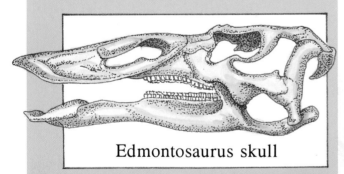

Edmontosaurus skull

It is easy to imagine a bird with a duckbill, but can you imagine a dinosaur with a duckbill? Well, there were several different kinds of dinosaurs with duckbills! They are called *Hadrosaurs*, meaning "big lizards." They are easily distinguished by their duckbills, but many also had bony crests or inflatable sacs of skin connected to their nostrils.

These medium-to large-sized dinosaurs were plant-eaters with strong jaws made for grinding and crushing plants and twigs. They had more teeth than any other dinosaur—up to 2000—that were diamond-shaped and designed to grind food as the jaws were closed. There were always new teeth growing underneath to replace the worn-out ones.

The hadrosaurs were bird-footed and bird-hipped. They probably depended on their keen eyes, ears, and nostrils for their best defense. Their backs were strong, with a mass of bony rods that reinforced the vertebrae when they walked or ran. Their shorter front legs, or arms, were probably used only when browsing for lower vegetation.

Edmontosaurus (ed-MON-toh-SORE-us), named for Edmonton, the area of Canada where the first remains were found, was one of the largest hadrosaurs: about 43 feet long and weighing 3–3½ tons. He looked similar to *Iguanodon* except for his broad duckbill and the lack of a spiked thumb on his hands.

From his nostrils to the top of his head was an area of loose skin that he could inflate. They probably lived in large herds where the males may have looked out for the safety of females and their young. These duckbills could well have been prey for the large meat-eating dinosaurs.

Two remarkable fossils of *Edmontosaurus* found in Wyoming showed what the skin of these dinosaurs looked like. These creatures had been buried so quickly that their flesh did not have time to decay before they were completely buried in the mud. This mud formed a mold around these dinosaurs, and left an impression of exactly what they were like, including the skin.

These impressions show that these dinosaurs had no armor or hard scales of any kind for protection. It appears that they had a skin much like the modern day lizard known as a Gila monster.

Tsintaosaurus (SEN-tou-SORE-us), called "Chinese lizard" because it was first found in China, had a unicorn-type horn projecting forward from between its eyes. The function of this hollow, skin-covered spike-like crest is uncertain, but perhaps it helped to amplify sound when he called.

The length of the *Tsintaosaurus* was about 33 feet. It had a toothless beak with a massive set of cheek teeth for chewing.

● Edmontosaurus

39

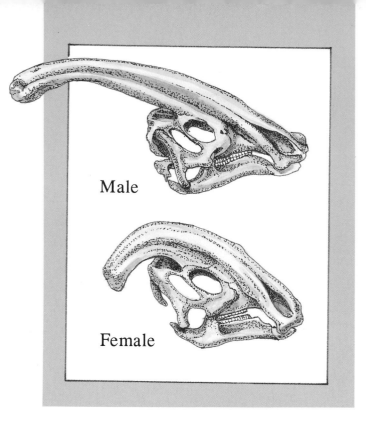

Male

Female

Corythosaurus (*coh-RITH-oh-SORE-us*) was known as the "helmeted lizard." The disk-shaped, bony crest that distinguished them was more prominent on the males than females. It was filled with a complex system of tubes probably used for breathing. No doubt it was also helpful in wedging a path through shrubs and thickets to find the desired food for its lunch.

Fossils of *Corythosaurus* indicate its size varied from 18– to 33–feet long and weighed from 2–4 tons. His skin had a pebble-like surface, feeling somewhat like a basketball. Around his belly were three rows of nodules.

Lambeosaurus (*LAM-bee-oh-SORE-us*) was named in honor of Canadian paleontologist Lawrence Lambe. It was perhaps the longest Ornithiscian (bird-hipped) dinosaur, about 40–49 feet long. The hatchet-like spike atop his head was his most distinguishing feature. This bony crest started from his nose and rose into a high crown above his eyes with a pointed handle extending backwards from his skull. A large cavity in this crest was connected to his nasal passage. The males' crests were probably larger.

This one was probably a faster runner than other duckbills. His limbs were relatively short, but he had powerful hind legs.

Parasaurolophus (*PAIR-ah-SORE-ol-OH-fus*), which means "like a crested lizard," had probably the most unusual of crests. It was a long, curved bony tube that extended way out behind his head.

Because only a few remains of *Parasaurolophus* have been found (all in North America), not much more is known about him. It is supposed he was 30–33 feet long and weighed around 5 tons. His tail was flattened and comparatively broad. He certainly was a conspicuous dinosaur.

No one really knows what purpose was served by the bony crests on many of the duck-billed dinosaurs. Scientists have offered several different ideas. The bony structures on all of these dinosaurs were hollow and were connected to their noses by tubes. We don't know either, but later on when we talk about "dragons," we are going to make an interesting suggestion.

o Corythosaurus

▲ Lambeosaurus

□ Tsintaosaurus

■ Parasaurolophus

41

Bone-Headed & Parrot-Like Dinosaurs

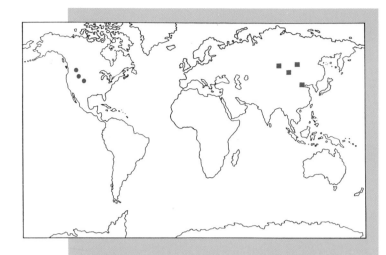

Family:

Pachycephalosauridae (thick-headed lizards)
  Pachycephalosaurus

Psittacosauridae (parrot lizards)
  Psittacosaurus

Fossil Locations:

Alberta, Canada; Wyoming, USA; Mongolia, China; South Siberia

Diet:

Plants

Interesting Facts:

Pachycephalosaurus

• Small brain, sharp eyesight, keen sense of smell.

• Wide hip structures could be either to strengthen the backbone for battering acts or for giving birth to live young.

Psittacosaurus

• Mongolian specimens, 10 inches long, found in 1925, were not recognized until 1980 as fossilized baby *Psittacosaurus*.

• Beak had *self-sharpening* cutting edges for biting plants.

These two types of dinosaurs had one thing in common—their unusual heads.

The male *Pachycephalosaurus* (*PACK-ee-CEF-ah-loh-SORE-us*) had a 9–inch-thick bone between the brain and the outer surface of the skull adorning the top of his head. They probably competed for supremacy of the flock by banging their bony crowns. The females had smaller boneheads.

They were about 15 feet in length, although some larger ones have been found. Their skulls—up to 26 inches long—were designed to transfer the shock of impact through the dome and around the sides of the head to the backbone.

Psittacosaurus (*sie-TACK-oh-SORE-us*) was so-named because of the parrot-like beak on its face. The first fossils found in Mongolia caused scientists to believe they were related to horned dinosaurs; *Psittacosaurus* had only small cheek horns and a bone under the upper beak like the horned dinosaurs.

The full grown ones were about 5 to 6½ feet long and weighed about 50 pounds.

They had a square-shaped skull with a large beak at the front of the mouth where there were no front teeth.

● Pachycephalosaurus

■ Psittacosaurus

Meat-Eating Dinosaurs

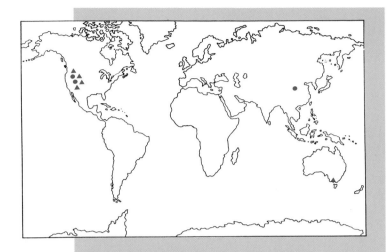

Family:
Allosauridae (different lizards)
Allosaurus
Tyrannosauridae (tyrant lizards)
Tyrannosaurus

Fossil Locations:
North America; Africa; Australia; China

Diet:
Meat

Interesting Facts:
- Fossils of duck-billed dinosaurs were found near the fossils of a *Tyrannosaurus*.
- Tyrannosaurs had binocular vision, which means they probably had very good depth perception.

The giant killers of the dinosaur world were carnivores. They were lizard-hipped theropods—dinosaurs that had bird-like feet with three long toes pointing forward, and a small dewclaw pointing backward.

Among the meat-eaters, there were different kinds of carnivores. Some attacked and killed the animals they could catch, either alone or in packs; some were scavengers that ate dead animals. This certainly isn't the world God desired when He placed all the animals in the Garden of Eden.

From the dinosaur bones and skeletons found in western Canada, it was determined that there were about 100 plant-eaters for every three to five meat-eaters. It's not hard to estimate how many plant-eaters were devoured to satisfy the hunger of the meat-eaters!

Imagine the scene as a hungry *Allosaurus* suddenly spots an *Apatosaurus* feeding on

▲ **Allosaurus**

plants along the shore of a lake. The *Allosaurus* is hunting for his intended victim as quietly as his huge size permits. Finally, when he is as near to *Apatosaurus* as possible without being seen, he suddenly lunges forward with the greatest speed possible.

Apatosaurus, caught by surprise, does not have time to seek the safety of deeper water. He has time only to make a few desperate defensive moves. He is not made for fighting, for he has no claws, and his teeth are not long and sharp like those of *Allosaurus*, but are short and flat for eating plants.

He is very big, however, and has a very large and powerful tail. As *Allosaurus* charges, he swings his huge tail at *Allosaurus* as quickly and powerfully as he can, hoping to knock *Allosaurus* off his feet. This would give

him time to flee to deeper water, or would perhaps give him an opportunity to crush or cripple *Allosaurus* by crashing his huge body down on this enemy.

But *Apatosaurus* is too slow. Before his thrashing tail can knock *Allosaurus* flat, *Allosaurus* has leaped upon his back, with his claws sinking deep into the flesh of *Apatosaurus*. The teeth of *Allosaurus* flash as he opens his huge jaws, and with one powerful snap he sinks his teeth deep into the neck of *Apatosaurus,* almost completely cutting through his spinal cord.

Thrashing wildly, *Apatosaurus* falls as *Allosaurus* again and again slashes at his

throat. Finally, *Apatosaurus* lies still and lifeless.

Allosaurus begins his feast, tearing away huge chunks of flesh and gulping greedily. When he has gorged himself, he slowly leaves the scene, seeking some cool spot to rest and sleep until hunger once again calls him to the hunt.

Allosaurus (*AL-oh-SORE-us*) was one of the best known carnivores. He was as large as a bus, 35–40 feet long, about 15 feet high, and weighed 1–2 tons. His most recognizable trait was probably his large 3-foot-long head, which was adorned with bumps and ridges.

No one could forget his mouth if they saw it opened. There were 40 long blade-sharp teeth (up to 4½ inches long) on top and 32 on the bottom, curving inward to help direct the meat into his body. His jaws were hinged at the very back of his massive head, and his skull had big holes on the sides so when he opened his mouth, it could expand sideways to take in huge chunks of meat. His large eye sockets indicate he also had very good vision!

In 1940, an excavation in Utah found the bones of some 40–60 allosaurs buried together. Scientists cannot be sure what catastrophe caused so many to die together, but the Great Flood of Noah's time is no doubt the best explanation.

Tyrannosaurus (*tie-RAN-oh-SORE-us*) is not only the most famous of dinosaurs, but it is also the largest carnivore. They stood 20 feet tall and were 50 feet long and weighed 6 or 7 tons—as large as a big semi-truck with a trailer! They certainly made a BIG impression with their skulls up to 6 feet long, and their 24-inch footprints. No wonder this dinosaur is called *Tyrannosaurus rex*, "king of the tyrant lizards."

He was bigger than *Allosaurus*, but had one noticeable difference—his arms were much shorter. No one has figured out just what he did with his weak little arms. They weren't long enough to even reach his chin and only had two fingers. His body build suggests he spent a lot of time laying down so they may have allowed him to raise up off the ground and brace himself while he moved his rear legs into position to stand up.

Until recently, much of what was known about *Tyrannosaurus* came from only seven incomplete skeletons and fragments. However, a nearly complete fossil skeleton was discovered recently on a ranch on the Cheyenne River Sioux Reservation near Faith, South Dakota. At the present time, a fierce legal battle is being fought over ownership of this fossil, valued up to five million dollars. Only one or two sets of footprints have been found in one place, which may mean that these beasts did not hunt in packs. Because of his size, he could run fast, but for only a very short distance. Some scientists believe he may have been somewhat of a scavenger, eating carrion (animals already dead) as much as he was a hunter. But his three-dimensional vision would certainly have enabled him to find his prey when on the prowl.

His teeth were enormous. The front fangs were as long as 7 inches, and his jaws could expand like *Allosaurus'* jaws. The brain cavity in his skull is smaller than his largest tooth. He was better equipped with brawn than brains!

Actual Size of
Tyrannosaurus
Tooth

● Tyrannosaurus

49

The Terrible Claws

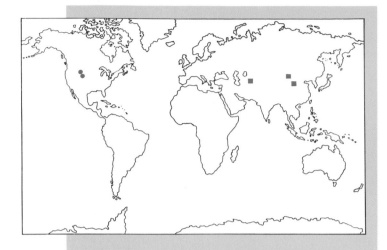

Family:
Dromaeosauridae (running lizards)
Deinonychus
Velociraptor

Fossil Locations:
Montana, Wyoming, USA; Mongolia; Kazakhstan

Diet:
Meat

Interesting Facts:
- Much of their length was composed of very stiff tails held rigid by narrow, bony rods extending from the tailbone, enabling them to run swiftly.
- Their remains have been found in groups, indicating that they probably roamed in packs and together attacked one large plant-eater.
- *Tenontosaurus* (teh-NON-toh-SORE-us) bones were found with those of several Deinonychus skeletons.
- Story of a *Velociraptor* life-and-death struggle forever locked in stone (page 18).

Meat-eaters were usually endowed with a variety of vicious-looking, sharp, curved claws for holding down their prey while blade-like teeth ripped chunks of meat from their victims. The most menacing of all were the terrible sickle-shaped "switchblade" claws of these dromaeosaurs.

Their forelimbs had three long claws on their fingers for grasping, but the strong hind legs had four toes. The first toe was small and turned backward, the third and fourth toes were strong enough to hold up the animal's weight when standing or running—all were well clawed; but the second toe with the long terrible claw was held high until ready to attack, when it could be flicked forward, slicing into the hide and flesh of its prey like a scalpel.

Deinonychus (*die-NON-ick-us*)—the "terrible claw"—was first found in the badlands of Montana, and greatly impressed his finders with his strong body, powerful jawbones, blade-like teeth, and the terrible 5-inch claws on his second toes. The full grown animals measured 10–12 feet long, were about 5 feet high, and probably weighed about 150–170 pounds.

The many large holes in his skull made it lightweight. He also must have had big eyes with excellent vision and a large brain. It is supposed that he could hold down his victim with one of his strong legs and, balanced by his rigid tail, use the claw on the other foot to cut out a chunk of meat. His 70 sharp, backward slanted teeth finished the work of having dinner.

Velociraptor (*vel-OS-ih-RAP-tore*), was the "swift robber" whose agility as a predator earned him the name. He had all the features of *Deinonychus*, except he was smaller and had a low, flat, narrow head and snout. He stood about 5 feet tall, was 6 feet long, and weighed about 150 pounds.

Very unusual for dinosaurs, he had collar bones which gave more strength to his forelimbs.

Tenantosaurus

● Deinonychus

■ Velociraptor

Big Plant-Eaters

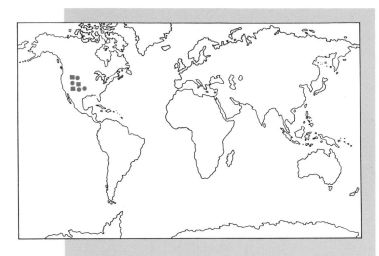

Family:

Brachiosauridae (arm lizards)
Brachiosaurus
Ultrasaurus
Diplodocidae (double beams)
Apatosaurus
Diplodocus
Supersaurus

Fossil Locations:

Colorado, Oklahoma, Utah, Montana,
Wyoming USA; Tanzania
Supersaurus: Colorado, USA
Ultrasaurus: Colorado, USA

Sauropods (lizard feet) were the largest—longest, tallest, heaviest—of all land animals. The blue whale has held the title of the "largest," but it is now being challenged by recent discoveries of some bones that may place dinosaurs in the lead.

These giants had rib bones as long as 6½ feet and as thick as a man's upper arm. They formed a barrel shape around the dinosaur's lungs, heart, and other vital organs. This made their bodies massive and bulky, but their long necks topped with tiny heads and long tails were more slender. Their strong legs were like tree trunks holding up this enormous weight and were postioned right under the heaviest part of their bodies. Their bones were designed for strength more than speed.

Many small stones, ranging from 2 to 5 inches long, have been found in dinosaur beds. Sometimes they appear right in the stomach area of a whole skeleton. These are believed to be gastroliths—stomach stones

used for grinding tough stalks and leaves for digestibility.

Diplodocus (*die-PLOH-dah-kus*) is one of the best known dinosaurs. It was a very long animal, thinner than other sauropods. Its length was about 87 feet, but it probably weighed no more than 10–12 tons. From the bones found so far, scientists give its measurements as: neck–27 feet long, tail–46 feet long, and body–16 feet high at hips.

Its tiny skull had 2 large eye sockets on each side, near the back of its head. There were no teeth in its mouth, except for one row of pencil-like pegs across the front of its jawbone, useable only for snipping off twigs and plants. It depended on stones for grinding up food in its stomach. At the top of the skull, above the eyes, was a large hole for the nostrils. Scientists are still puzzled by these unusual skulls.

The backbone was designed to allow the animal to raise its forelimbs off the ground. This was no doubt helpful in reaching the tops of trees. His tail was very long, thin, and flexible—probably used with a sharp whiplash effect whenever needed as a weapon. In addition, its legs were very strong should a pounce on a hungry predator be necessary.

Its name, meaning "double beam," comes from the little skids on the middle tail bones, which may have been to shield the blood vessels when the long tail dragged behind.

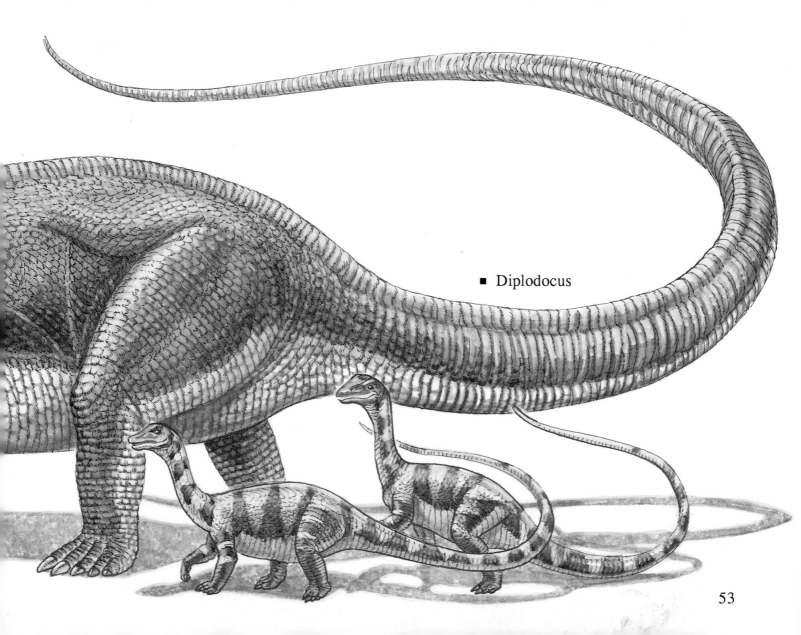

■ Diplodocus

Top: Camarasaurus-type skull

Bottom: Diplodocus-type skull

Apatosaurus (*uh-PAT-oh-SORE-us*) was called the "deceptive reptile." The name "deceptive" is well chosen due to the confusion its fossils caused. In 1877, Othniel Marsh gave the name *Apatosaurus* to a dinosaur whose hip and back bone fossils were found in a quarry near Morrison, Colorado. Over the next few years, more fossils of *Apatosaurus* were found, including fragments of a skull.

In 1879, Marsh gave the name *Brontosaurus* to an almost complete skeleton, found at Como Bluff, Wyoming, which was missing its skull. Marsh later reconstructed the skeleton of this "Brontosaurus," but gave it a square-shaped *Camarasaurus*-type skull that had been found in a different quarry, and in a different layer of strata.

In 1975 Dr. Jack McIntosh and Dr. David Berman convinced the scientific community that *Apatosaurus* and *Brontosaurus* were the same animal, and that *Apatosaurus* had a skull exactly like that of *Diplodocus*.

Since the rules used for giving scientific names to animals state that the first name given is the one kept, the name *Apatosaurus* stayed and *Brontosaurus* was dropped.

The confusion remains today as you can see by the "Brontosaurus" stamp issued by the U. S. Postal Service in 1989.

Apatosaurus was a massive animal. The 82 bones in its tail balanced its 20-foot-long neck with its small, low head. Its overall length was 76 feet, its body height was about 17 feet at the hips and 14 feet at the shoulders. With flesh and muscle on such a skeleton, scientists estimate it probably weighed 30–42 tons.

In Texas, there are 23 sets of footprints believed to have been made by *Apatosaurus*. Each one is about 39 inches long, with no

● Apatosaurus

55

sign of a tail dragging behind so it was either walking in water with the tail floating at the time, or carried its tail in the air. Along with these prints were also those of a herd of three-toed dinosaurs—meat-eaters! Some of these footprints were underneath the prints of *Apatosaurus* and some were on top. Perhaps these were made by *Allosaurus*.

Tail bones of an *Apatosaurus* found in one location showed grooves from teeth marks exactly matching teeth in the jaw of an *Allosaurus* found buried with it. Some loose teeth of the predator were also lying around. There had apparently been a vicious fight previous to their deaths.

Brachiosaurus (*BRAK-ee-oh-SORE-us*) was called the "arm lizard" because it had long forelimbs that held its shoulders higher than its hips. The shoulders of a full grown *Brachiosaurus* stood 16–19 feet from the ground. It made a slanted line downward from his head, past his shoulders and hips, to his tail. His body was probably more bulky than other sauropods. In fact, it was the tallest dinosaur, until recent findings that may provide evidence of a still larger variety.

Brachiosaurus was first identified from some bones found in Colorado in 1900. About a decade later, when 250 tons of dinosaur bones were obtained from Tanzania, a complete skeleton of a *Brachiosaurus* was among them, and was later reconstructed in a Berlin museum. It is still the largest mounted dinosaur skeleton in the world. It is 75 feet long, 39 feet high, and can hold its head over 42 feet in the air. It probably weighed about

75 tons or more. Certainly this was the giraffe of the dinosaur world.

His head was very small, with a broad nose and chisel-shaped teeth at the front of its mouth. A most unusual feature of *Brachiosaurus* was the fact that its nostrils were not located on the end of its snout, but in the hollow dome on the top of its head. Scientists originally thought that it could submerge itself in water and leave only its nostrils above the water level, but this has since been discounted because his lungs and body could not have withstood the pressure in water as deep as 40 feet. Its neck was heavy and strong.

The tail was somewhat shorter and thicker than other dinosaurs. The backbone vertebrae design was deeply hollowed on the sides, looking somewhat like an I-beam such as is used in constructing big buildings.

Ultrasaurus (*UL-tra-SORE-us*) was named "ultra" from a few large bones found not long ago. After examining shoulder blade bones 9 feet long, scientists estimated this animal was about 100 feet long and weighed as much as 100–150 tons. A dinosaur this size would need 4–5 tons of plant food every day. Standing on the ground, he could look into the fifth floor windows of a tall building.

The truth is, no one knows very much about this dinosaur because so few bones have been found. They resemble the bones of *Brachiosaurus*, so it is presumed this animal must have been built much like him. No scientific name has been given yet. It may be smaller than the other new dinosaur recently

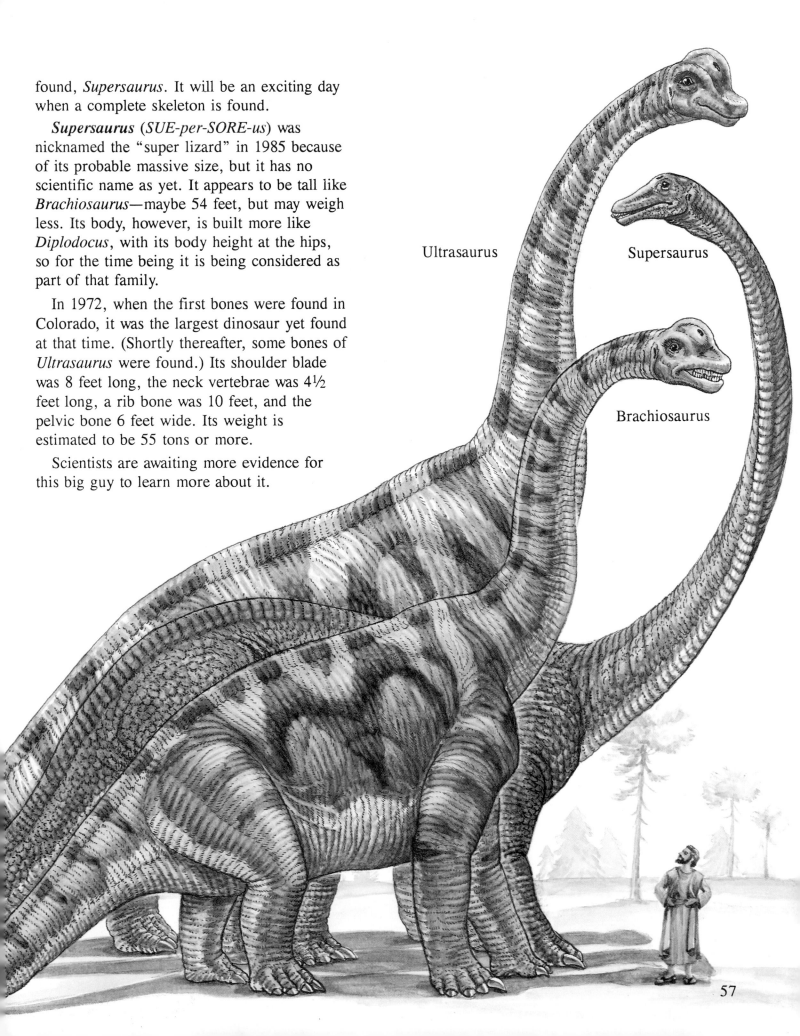

found, *Supersaurus*. It will be an exciting day when a complete skeleton is found.

Supersaurus (*SUE-per-SORE-us*) was nicknamed the "super lizard" in 1985 because of its probable massive size, but it has no scientific name as yet. It appears to be tall like *Brachiosaurus*—maybe 54 feet, but may weigh less. Its body, however, is built more like *Diplodocus*, with its body height at the hips, so for the time being it is being considered as part of that family.

In 1972, when the first bones were found in Colorado, it was the largest dinosaur yet found at that time. (Shortly thereafter, some bones of *Ultrasaurus* were found.) Its shoulder blade was 8 feet long, the neck vertebrae was 4½ feet long, a rib bone was 10 feet, and the pelvic bone 6 feet wide. Its weight is estimated to be 55 tons or more.

Scientists are awaiting more evidence for this big guy to learn more about it.

Ultrasaurus

Supersaurus

Brachiosaurus

57

Flying Reptiles

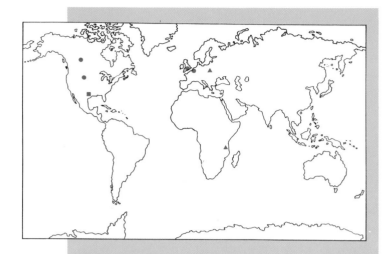

Family:

Azhdarchidae
Quetzalcoatlus
Pteranodontidae
Pteranodon
Rhamphorhynchidae
Rhamphorhynchus

Fossil Locations:

Texas, Wyoming, USA; Alberta, Canada; England; North Europe; Bavaria; Africa

Diet:

Fish, larval crustaceans, insects

Interesting Facts:

- Now believed to have been efficient flyers.
- *Pteranodon* wing membrane strengthened by tiny fibers (aktinofibrils) .002 inches thick.
- Some *Pteranodon* fossils suggest they had a coat of fine hair.

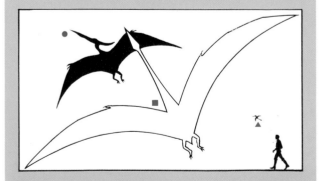

Although they weren't dinosaurs, there were other kinds of rather frightening creatures that lived at the same time with dinosaurs. Apparently they all died out some time after the Flood, just as the dinosaurs did. These were the flying reptiles.

All flying reptiles had one very long finger (the fourth finger on each hand). Their bat-like wings consisted of a leathery membrane that stretched between the long finger and the body. These flying reptiles were *very* different from birds. Scientists used to think flying reptiles could fly only by gliding. They thought the flying reptiles had to climb to the top of a cliff and jump off, catching a warm updraft of air to fly. Can you imagine all these animals going mountain climbing? Many scientists have now changed their minds and think they were active fliers.

Tiny **Rhamphorhynchus** (*ram-fo-RINK-us*) was only about 1½ feet long. It had a long, narrow skull and teeth that pointed forward (probably good for spearing fish). Its long tail had a kite-shaped rudder on the end. Like all flying reptiles, it had light weight hollow bones.

Pteranodon (*tair-AN-o-don*) had a bony crest that went backward from the skull. Its average wingspan was 23 feet, and looked quite spectacular on its 3-foot body—about the size of a turkey. The wings and the body together weighed only about 44 pounds.

Quetzalcoatlus (*ket-sol-ko-AT-lus*) was named after a mythical Aztec god. The largest known animals ever to fly, they possibly flew low over the ocean to scoop up fish that were swimming just under the surface. One *Quetzalcoatlus* fossil was discovered in Big Bend National Park, Texas, in 1972, and had a wingspread of nearly 48 feet. That's longer than the wingspread of a F-4 Phantom jet!

▲ Rhamphorhynchus

● Pteranodon

■ Quetzalcoatlus

Marine Reptiles

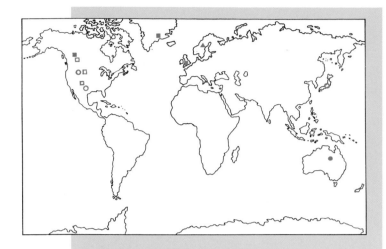

Family:

    Ichthyosauridae
        Ichthyosaurus
        Ophthalmosaurus
    Plesiosauridae
        Elasmosaurus
    Pliosauridae
        Kronosaurus

Fossil Locations:

    Texas, Wyoming, South Dakota,USA; Alberta, Canada; Australia; Japan; Norway; Greenland; England

Diet:

    Meat

Interesting Facts:

    • Efficient swimmers.
    • Reptiles that lived in the sea.

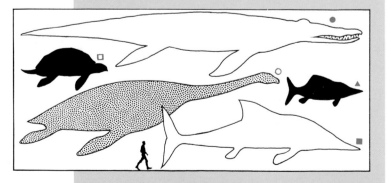

When dinosaurs lived on earth, there were not only strange reptiles flying in the sky, but there were also some very unusual reptiles living in the ocean. Many of these marine reptiles died during the Flood because of turbulence and sedimentation in the water.

Elasmosaurus (*ee-LASS-moh-SORE-us*) had a neck that was more than half of its 43-foot length. He had a small head that was filled with sharp teeth to catch fish near the surface of the water. He may have been one of the lucky ones to have made it through the Flood. Many people believe the *Elasmosaurus* is not only the "sea monster" sailors have been seeing since ancient times, but he may also be the famous "Loch Ness Monster."

Ichthyosaurus (*ICK-thee-oh-SORE-us*) was a very fast swimmer with its streamlined body. He could have been the acrobat of the sea, just like the dolphins of today. From fossil remains it appears they gave birth to live babies. He grew to be 10 feet long.

Ophthalmosaurus (*op-THAL-moe-SORE-us*), or "eye reptile," is an ichthyosaurian with eyes the size of saucers. He must have been at least 12 feet long because its skull was nearly 3½ feet in length.

Kronosaurus (*KROH-no-SORE-us*) could truly be called "Jaws." He would be a scuba diver's worst nightmare! This monster grew to be 56 feet long. His jaw was over 10 feet long and filled with bullet-shaped teeth that measured 10 inches in length. He could dive very deeply, but because he was a reptile, he needed to come up for air.

Archelon (*AR-kee-lon*) was a large turtle that grew to be 14 feet long. Its fossils have been found in South Dakota. It may have used its hooked beak to eat shellfish.

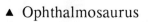

▲ Ophthalmosaurus

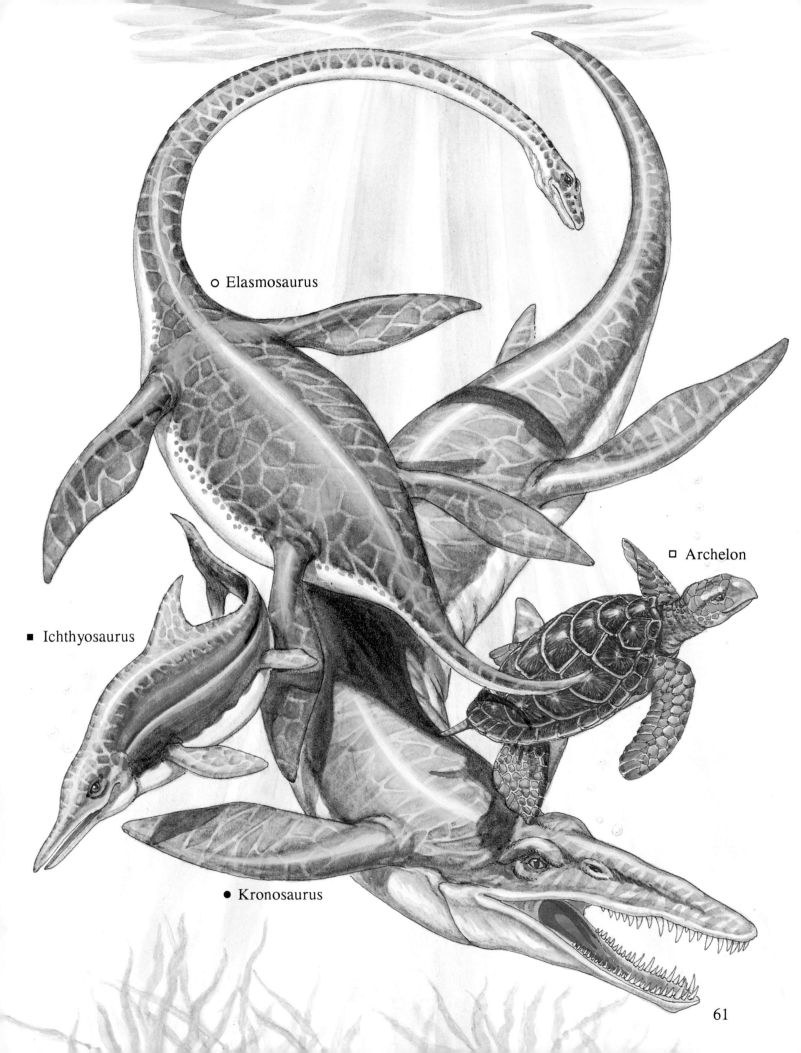

o Elasmosaurus

■ Ichthyosaurus

□ Archelon

● Kronosaurus

61

Evolutionary Fairy Tales

If you asked an evolutionist to describe from what the dinosaurs evolved, he wouldn't know how to answer. No one has ever found even a trace of an ancestor for any of the dinosaurs, flying reptiles, or marine reptiles. Creationists, of course, believe that God created them just the way they were on earth.

Evolutionists assume that the flying reptiles evolved from some ordinary reptile—perhaps a lizard—that lived on the land. They suppose that this imaginary ancestor for the flying reptiles started out with the feet and legs of a lizard, or a lizard-like animal. Then, according to their imaginary evolutionary story, a strange thing happened. A genetic accident or mistake occurred in this lizard (these genetic accidents or mistakes are called mutations), causing one or more of the baby lizards, either fathered or mothered by the mutant lizard, to have fourth fingers that were just a wee bit longer than other lizards' fourth fingers.

Furthermore, evolutionists tell us, for some strange unknown reason, the lizards with slightly longer fourth fingers had an advantage over the lizards with ordinary fourth fingers. As a result, in the struggle for existence or the war for survival, the lizards with slightly longer fourth fingers reproduced in larger number than the lizards with ordinary fingers, so eventually the ordinary lizards all died out, leaving only the ones with the longer fourth fingers. Then after a few hundred years, or perhaps a few thousand years and a lot of bad mutations which produced crippled or diseased lizards that all died out, another good mutation made the fourth fingers get just a wee bit longer again. Once again, the struggle for existence resulted in a dying out of the lizards with shorter fingers. Thus, we are told, the fourth fingers got longer and longer and longer.

At the same time (would you believe it?) many other genetic mistakes or mutations somehow created the wing membranes, the flight muscles, changed their solid bones to hollow ones, and—in the case of *Pteranodon*—changed ordinary jaws and teeth into a long toothless beak. Finally, this creature became a flying reptile!

Now let's think about all of this for a moment. Let's imagine what would happen when this evolutionary process was incomplete. Consider a reptile whose wings have developed up to 25%. The poor creature obviously cannot fly with only a fourth of his wings, but he cannot run any more either! Such animals would certainly look funny, dragging those useless partial wings around when they tried to run. In that predicament they could no longer run fast enough to catch something to eat nor run away fast enough to escape other animals who wanted to eat them. So what would the result be? Why, they would soon be eliminated, of course. We can only conclude that belief in such a process of gradual evolution from a land reptile into a flying one is just too ridiculous.

These explanations of the evolution process are really fairy tales. Not one single fossil has been found of an animal in an intermediate

form between a land reptile and a flying reptile. The fossil record shows that every *Rhamphorhynchus* has always been *Rhamphorhynchus* and every *Pteranodon* has been a *Pteranodon* from their beginning. This is the way God created them.

The same is true of the marine reptiles. If ordinary land reptiles changed into marine reptiles, then one of those land reptiles must have ventured into the water; and after eons of time and a long series of genetic mistakes, it gradually changed into a fish-like reptile, or *Ichthyosaurus*. If this were true, we ought to find at least some in-between kinds. Perhaps an animal with feet and legs gradually changing into paddle-like fins would give evidence of this evolution. But not one such transitional form has ever been found!

Every one of the marine reptiles just popped into the fossil record fully formed at the very start. None are 25%, 50%, or 75% along the way; all are 100% complete. This is exactly what we would expect to find if God is the Creator of these creatures. These fossils give powerful evidence against evolution.

Ancestors of Birds?

Fossil hunters are very frustrated that they have not been able to find *any* transitional forms, or in-between kinds, that they should be able to find if evolution were true. Instead, each one of the many *kinds* of dinosaurs appear in the fossil record already complete, as if they came out of nowhere, just as you would expect if God had created them.

Dinosaurs come in all shapes and sizes; tall ones, short ones, fat ones, skinny ones. The list goes on and on, but no matter what they looked like on the outside, on the inside there are only two groups.

Ornithischians (*or-ni-THISS-ey-un*) are the "bird-hipped" dinosaurs. Bird-hipped dinosaurs ate mostly plants; some had horny beaks, and an extra bone at the lower jaw tip. Many of them lacked front teeth, but had powerful cheek teeth, and cheek pouches. Some of them also had bony tendons stiffening the spine.

Saurischians (*say-RISS-ey-un*) are the "lizard-hipped" dinosaurs. This group of dinosaurs included both plant and meat-eaters. Some had large holes in the skull which reduced the weight of its head. Most of the saurischians had teeth set in the outer rim of the jaw.

Each of these groups bear names that are derived from Greek words. That way, a paleontologist from Italy and a paleontologist from Canada can be sure that they are talking about the exact same dinosaur at scientific meetings or in technical writings.

The illustration on the bottom of the page show what these bones looked like. The dinosaurs had three bones on each side of the pelvis: the ilium, ischium, and the pubis. In reptile-hipped dinosaurs, the pubis pointed forward, and the ischium pointed backward. In bird-hipped dinosaurs, the pubis pointed backward with the ischium. You have just had a mini-anatomy lesson on dinosaurs.

Looking at the illustration, don't the ostrich and the *Struthiomimus* look a lot alike? Wouldn't *Struthiomimus* make a great in-between form between dinosaur and birds, especially if some feathers were added?

Unfortunately for evolution theory, there is something very wrong with this idea. *Struthiomimus* was not a *bird-hipped* dinosaur. Yes, you guessed it, he was a *lizard-hipped* dinosaur!

If evolution were true, you would expect dinosaurs with bird hips would look like birds, wouldn't you? *Ankylosaurus* looks more like a low-slung tank than a graceful airborne bird. What kind of hips does *Ankylosaurus* have? Right again, bird-hips.

In fact, all of the dinosaurs that had long slim legs, small lightweight bodies, and in general appearance looked somewhat like birds, were lizard-hipped. On the other hand, the dinosaurs that were bird-hipped were otherwise all wrong to be the ancestors for birds. These facts are difficult to understand for those who assume evolution is true, but they surely don't present any problems for scientists who believe in creation!

Furthermore, *Struthiomimus* and similar dinosaurs didn't have even a hint of a feather. All dinosaurs had ordinary reptile skin. *Archaeopteryx* is supposed to be one of the first birds. He had perfect feathers, just like birds living today. God made him that way!

Dinosaur Types Covered in this Book

Ornithischia (bird-hipped)

Iguanodon (24–25)
Horned Dinosaurs (28–31)
Plated Dinosaurs (32–35)
Armored Dinosaurs (36–37)
Duck-billed Dinosaurs (38–41)
Bone-headed & Parrot-like Dinosaurs (42–43)

Saurischia (lizard-hipped)

Lightweights (26–27)
Meat-eating Dinosaurs (44–49)
The Terrible Claws (50–51)
Big Plant-eaters (52–57)

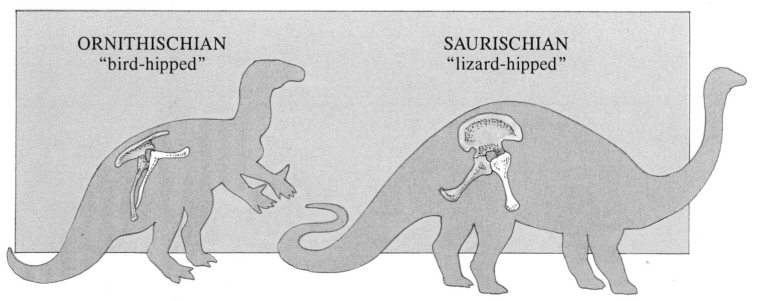

ORNITHISCHIAN
"bird-hipped"

SAURISCHIAN
"lizard-hipped"

Archaeopteryx

Birds are one of God's most wonderful creatures. They come in many sizes, shapes, colors, and unique characteristics. Best of all, most can fly free in the sky.

One of the birds God created— *Archaeopteryx* (*AR-kee-OP-ter-iks*)—is now extinct. Evolutionists believe that because *Archaeopteryx* had some "reptile-like" characteristics, it must be a "missing link" between reptiles and birds. But *Archaeopteryx* was very much a bird! It had perching feet, feathered wings (feathers identical to modern birds), a bird-like skull, and a furcula (wishbone). (No animals except birds have feathers.)

Archaeopteryx did have claws on its wings. This, however, doesn't mean it's a cousin to a lizard. Three birds living today have claws on their wings. The hoatzin, in South America, has claws when young. The touraco of Africa has claws, and the ostrich has three claws on each wing.

Feathers are marvels of complicated construction. They appear *suddenly* in the fossil record, and there is no evidence of feather evolution. The idea that feathers evolved from frayed-out scales is pure fantasy. Scales and feathers develop in an entirely different manner.

Feathers combine lightness, strength, and flexibility. They provide padding that protects the bird's thin, sensitive skin, and act as a thermal barrier, trapping body heat in the spaces between the fluffed feathers. Feathers are so efficient that they can keep the bird's temperature at a normal 106.7° F. in below-freezing temperatures.

There are four main types of feathers. Contour feathers cover the bird's body, giving it a streamlined shape. Down feathers are for temperature insulation. Filoplumes sometimes stick out from the coat and serve as a kind of decoration. Flight feathers are the long stiff feathers found on wings and tail.

A flight feather has a central shaft with a series of parallel barbs extending diagonally out from it on each side (see illustration). The barbs have small filaments, called barbules, branching off them, and the hooks on each filament lock on to other filaments to form a mesh. These hooks are so small they can't be seen with the naked eye. If the "mesh" comes apart, the bird draws the feather through its beak several times and the hooks remesh, just like a zipper. An eagle feather is incredibly strong, as each feather is held together by more than 250,000 tiny hooks.

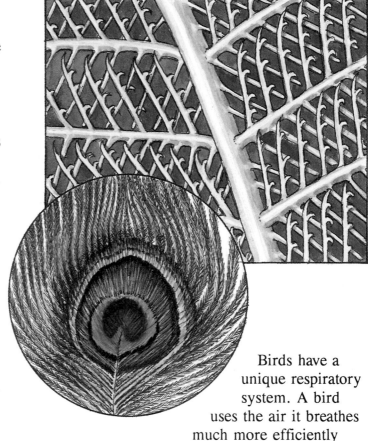

Some birds, like peacocks (round insert) and hummingbirds, have feathers that seem to be iridescent. If these feathers were magnified many times, you would see what looks like thousands of "bubbles." These bubbles have different shapes and thicknesses, enabling light to bounce off them at different angles. It is the light bouncing off at different angles that causes the multiple colors of their feathers. This is called refraction.

How many feathers does a bird have? As you might guess, quite a few. Someone once took the time to count every feather on a Plymouth Rock hen. There were 8,325. Another person plucked a whistling swan and counted 25,216 feathers. An average songbird will have between 1,100 and 4,600 feathers, and many birds even have seasonal feathers. A goldfinch may have 1,000 more feathers on its body in winter than in summer.

A bird's body is a model of efficiency. It combines low weight and great strength. There isn't an ounce of extra weight anywhere on its body. A bald eagle is a large bird with over 7,000 feathers. Yet, all of these feathers put together weigh less than 21 ounces.

In some birds, flight muscles account for half the bird's weight. The muscles that pull the wings down are by far the largest, because most of the power for flying is needed for the downward stroke.

Birds have a unique respiratory system. A bird uses the air it breathes much more efficiently than a rabbit, fox, or other mammal with larger lungs. God may have given birds small lungs, but he also gave them a marvelous system of air sacs. These air sacs can be found in every important part of the bird's body. Not only do the air sacs allow birds to get the most out of every breath, but they also act as temperature regulators.

God also gave birds superb eyesight. It would be pretty hard for a circling hawk to swoop down and grab a rabbit to feed the chicks back at the nest if he couldn't see it. One sensitive spot on the retina (called the fovea) has 1½ million visual cells. A man's eye at the same place has only 200,000.

We havn't even touched on many other wonderful design features God gave birds. We could have whole chapters on hollow bones, specialized beaks, and aerodynamics that make airplane designers green with envy. All this shows evidence of an incredibly intelligent designer, not the random happenings of time and chance.

Affects of Sin

In this book we have described dinosaurs that apparently ate meat. Many dinosaurs certainly had the proper equipment—teeth, jaws, and claws—to do so. We think they ate meat, but we cannot be absolutely sure that some dinosaurs ate other animals, even though they had the strength and teeth for it. Many animals today *look* like they would be meat-eaters—but aren't. A gorilla, for instance, has some fierce-looking teeth, but gorillas don't eat meat. They are *herbivores*; they eat only plants and fruits. There are some fruit-eating bats that have very sharp teeth. And what about the Giant Pandas? They have very sharp teeth that would seem just right for cutting up raw meat. But the main thing Giant Pandas like to eat is bamboo.

After God had created Adam and Eve and all the animals, He told them that they were to eat plants and fruits:

> And God said, "See, I have given you every herb that yields seed which is on the face of all the earth, and every tree whose fruit yields seed; to you it shall be for food. Also, to every beast of the earth, to every bird of the air, and to everything that creeps on the earth, in which there is life, I have given every green herb for food"; and it was so.

Genesis 1:29,30

It seems very clear that God commanded man and animals to eat only plants and fruits. Then why do you suppose dinosaurs ate the meat of other animals?

Let's review what happened. God had given Adam a clear command:

> And the Lord God commanded the man, saying, "Of every tree of the garden you may freely eat; but of the tree of the knowledge of good and evil you shall not eat, for in the day that you eat of it you shall surely die."

Genesis 2:16,17

What did Adam and Eve do? That's right, they did exactly what God had told them *not* to. Was the sin just in eating a piece of fruit? No, the sin was the *deliberate* disobedience of God's command.

As a result of this sin, selfishness, rebellion, and violence came into the world. Cain murdered Abel, his brother. People and animals began to disobey God in all their ways. They took what they wanted, did what they wanted, and ate what they wanted—regardless of God's commands.

> The earth also was corrupt before God, and the earth was filled with violence. So God looked upon the earth, and indeed it was corrupt; for all flesh had corrupted their way on the earth.

Genesis 6:11,12

Apparently, after Adam disobeyed God and sinned, all mankind began to live a rebellious, violent life. Animals also became violent, and many began to kill other animals for their own food. Because God knew all things from the beginning, He prepared some animals with armor and defensive weapons, like the horns and shields of *Triceratops* and the big sharp spikes on the tail of *Stegosaurus*. He gave an incredible defense system to the bombardier beetle, as we shall learn later. These were given for them to defend themselves.

Did God design the teeth, jaws, and claws of *Tyrannosaurus* and other meat-eating dinosaurs so these creatures could kill other animals and eat their meat? Not necessarily; many of these may have been designed originally for eating plants and fruit, just like the teeth of the Giant Panda, gorillas, and fruit-eating bats. No one knows for sure just how and why animals started eating meat, except that it was after the Fall.

Perhaps, after sin and violence came into the world, some animals became more ferocious, and developed an appetite for meat. Having the teeth, jaws, claws and the power to do so, these animals began to kill and eat other animals. We don't know for sure if this is the only correct explanation, or if some of these structures were designed for the purpose of hunting and eating other animals.

This was not the world God had originally designed. All the people, except for a man named Noah and his family, had become so corrupt that God decided to bring a great flood to destroy the earth and most of the people and animals that lived on the earth. After the Great Flood, God gave a new teaching regarding the eating of animal flesh. He told Noah,

> Every moving thing that lives shall be food for you. I have given you all things, even as the green herbs.
>
> *Genesis 9:3*

From that time on, God permitted man to include meat in his diet.

The Great Flood

The story of Noah and the Great Flood is one of the world's greatest dramas. God grieved over a sin-filled world whose people had rebelled against Him and brought worldwide judgment against the Creation.

Then the LORD saw that the wickedness of man was great in the earth, and that every intent of the thoughts of his heart was only evil continually.

And the LORD was sorry that He had made man on the earth, and He was grieved in His heart.

So the LORD said, "I will destroy man whom I have created from the face of the earth, both man and beast, creeping thing and birds of the air, for I am sorry that I have made them."

But Noah found grace in the eyes of the LORD.

Genesis 6:5–8

Just think what it must have been like for Noah and his family. No one else they knew believed in God—only Noah, his wife, his three sons (Shem, Ham and Japheth) and their wives. Only eight people in all the world believed in God and served Him.

Even before God gave Noah the order to build the Ark, his neighbors must have considered him to be old-fashioned and boring—definitely not someone who knew how to have a "good time." Can you imagine what they thought after he began building an Ark on dry land? Serving God is not always easy, but Noah wanted God's approval more than that of his neighbors.

God was going to save Noah and his family from the coming destruction, so He gave Noah specific instructions on how to do his part. Noah not only followed God's instructions to the letter, but he also worked faithfully on the Ark for 120 years.

God told Noah the Ark was to be:

- Made of gopher wood (cypress)
- Treated with pitch to make it watertight
- 300 cubits long (438 feet)
- 50 cubits wide (73 feet)
- 30 cubits high (44 feet)
- Equipped with a window across the top 1 cubit high
- Fitted with a door on the side
- 3 levels high inside

A cubit (means the *forearm*) is believed to be the distance between a man's elbow and the end of his fingers. Usually the measurement of 17½ inches is used for calculations.

Noah was about to become the first curator of the first known zoo. Not only was the Ark for Noah and his family, but he was to take on board huge numbers of animals. Again God was very specific in his instructions to Noah. He was to have a male and female of every living creature (yes, that means dinosaurs, too). He was to have 2 (in some cases 14) of every land animal, including birds and all the creepy crawleys.

Now, before you imagine Noah going on great safaris, know that God told Noah He would bring all of the animals to the Ark. For the God who created these animals and all of their instincts, it would have been easy for Him to tell each one to migrate there.

That must have been quite a sight for all the people to see. You would think at least some of the neighbors would wonder if Noah was right about God and they were wrong. Even if they wondered, they did nothing about it or they would have been on the Ark, too.

You may wonder how Noah got all those animals on the Ark. With a shoehorn? The Ark was *much* larger than you would think! It was shaped like a barge (for stability in rough water), as long as 1½ football fields, and taller than a four-story building. It would hold as much as 533 railroad stock cars, and had a volume of 1,396,000 cubic feet.

The Ark was gigantic, and designed to accomodate the large number of animals God intended it to hold. There were many small animals and insects, but consider also that there were some large animals. It seems likely that God would send young animals instead of full-grown versions of the larger species. A young *Apatosaurus* would take up a lot less room than an adult.

Next problem—the care (stall-cleaning, etc.) and feeding of so many animals. And, don't forget there's the matter of how to keep the *Tyrannosaurus* from nibbling on his nearest neighbor. Again, not a problem for God. The God who created them could have very easily have put most or all of them into a form of hibernation. Hibernation can be described as "a state in which normal functions are suspended or greatly retarded, enabling the animal to endure long periods of complete inactivity."

Next comes one of the most exciting scriptures in the Bible. Once Noah, his family, and the animals were in the Ark,

> ... and the LORD shut him in.
>
> *Genesis 7:16*

This is a beautiful picture of how God provided safety (salvation) in the face of certain destruction. Sin had entered the world and had to be punished. Today we are facing the same choice. Do we choose sin or do we choose God?

God promised to never again destroy the world with a world-wide flood, so He won't be ordering any more arks built. Instead, He sent His own Son, Jesus Christ, to be *our* salvation. Jesus died on the cross to pay for our sins so we wouldn't have to. Jesus took our punishment—He is our Ark.

How do you receive this salvation? Admit to yourself and to God that you have sinned, and ask His forgiveness. Then ask Jesus to come into your heart and be your Lord and Savior. Salvation is a free gift, bought and paid for, but you must ask for it.

Jesus gives a beautiful promise to those who have accepted Him:

> My sheep hear My voice, and I know them, and they follow Me. And I give them eternal life, and they shall never perish; neither shall anyone snatch them out of My hand. My Father, who has given them to Me, is greater than all; and no one is able to snatch them out of My Father's hand.
>
> *John 10:27-29*

Just as Jesus keeps us safe today, Noah and all in the Ark were kept safe as things started getting pretty rough.

> ... on that day all the fountains of the great deep were broken up, and the windows of heaven were opened. And the rain was on the earth forty days and forty nights.
>
> *Genesis 7:11,12*

For forty days and nights the flood waters kept rising until all the mountains were covered. There must have been great tidal waves during this time. In God's design, the Ark was planned for stability, not for going great distances. All the Ark needed to do was stay afloat. If the animals were hibernating, they would have slept through the whole thing.

The water covered the earth for 150 days, and nothing was left alive that had lived on the earth or in the air before the Flood. Many of the fish and animals in the ocean would have perished also. Through all of this, God kept Noah, his family, and all of the animals safe from harm.

God sent a wind to help dry up the waters, and after ten months the tops of the mountains became visible. Noah first sent a raven out of the window atop the Ark, but it did not return. Next he sent a dove, but the dove found no tree or place to rest, so it returned to the Ark. Noah was still trusting the Lord and knew it wasn't time yet. A week later he sent the dove again, and it returned with an olive leaf in its beak. The following week it did not return at all, so Noah knew there was some dry land where the dove could stay.

Noah and his family lived on that Ark for 53 weeks, until God told him to leave the Ark and let all the animals go. He wanted them to begin replenishing the earth with more people and animals.

The first thing Noah did was build an altar and thank God for His protection. Looking around the Ark at the desolation, he had to have been shocked at the changes that had taken place. He realized how good God had been to him and his family.

God promised Noah and his family that He would never again destroy the earth with a flood, and He gave the rainbow to remind mankind of that promise.

The earth they found was nothing like the one they had been used to before the Flood. There were no forests or great herds of animals. Where there were probably gentle rolling hills before, now there stood high mountains. Instead of an even climate, there were great temperature changes. No, this was not the world they had left, and it would never be the same again.

Flood Legends

Evidences of a worldwide flood can be found in the more than 270 flood stories and historic records found in many parts of the world. Flood legends are common in the folk tales of many other countries. Their various interpretations reflect the way details may change when stories are told from one generation to another because of the absence of written records available to them. Let's look at just a few of these stories.

Hawaii

Long after the death of Kuniuhonna, the first man, the world became a wicked, terrible place to live. There was one good man left; his name was Nu-u.

He made a great canoe with a house on it and filled it with animals. The waters came up over all the earth and killed all the people. Only Nu-u and his family were saved.

China

Ancient Chinese writings refer to a violent catastrophe that happened to the Earth. They report that the entire land was flooded. The water went up to the highest mountains and completely covered all the foothills. It left the country in desolate condition for years after.

One ancient Chinese classic called the "Hihking" tells the story of Fuhi, whom the Chinese consider to be the father of their civilization. This history records that Fuhi, his wife, three sons, and three daughters escaped a great flood. He and his family were the only people left alive on earth. After the great flood they repopulated the world.

An ancient temple in China has a wall painting that shows Fuhi's boat in the raging waters. Dolphins are swimming around the boat and a dove with an olive branch in its beak is flying toward it.

Toltec

Found in the histories of the Toltec Indians of ancient Mexico is a story of the first world that lasted 1,716 years and was destroyed by a great flood that covered even the highest mountains. Their story tells of a few men who escaped the destruction in a "toptlipetlocali," which means a closed chest. Following the great flood, these men began to multiply and built a very high "zacuali," or a great tower, to provide a safe place if the world were destroyed again. However, the languages became confused, so different language groups wandered to other parts of the world.

The Toltecs claim they started as a family of seven friends and their wives who spoke the same language. They crossed great waters, lived in caves, and wandered 104 years till they came to Hue Hue Tlapalan (southern Mexico). The story reports that this was 520 years after the great flood.

Babylonia

Other than the record found in the Bible, the most ancient account of the Great Flood, also called the Deluge, is a tablet inscription found in Babylonia. The tablet referred to an older tablet from which this was copied, but only fragments have been found of that older copy, which was handed down from a previous king of Babylon. Because many people lived several hundred years at that time, the account of the Flood could easily have been reported by someone like King Amraphel (Genesis 14:1), who was one of the early kings of Babylonia after the Flood.

Another flood account was prevalent during the time of Alexander the Great, probably recorded by a Babylonian historian for the benefit of the Greeks. He wrote of the ante-diluvian (pre-flood) rulers and of the "great Deluge" that covered the earth.

What Happened to the Dinosaurs?

No one really knows why all the dinosaurs became extinct. Scientists have thought a lot about this question, but have never been able to find a completely satisfactory answer. Many suggestions have been made, but only one seems to fit most of the facts.

Some have suggested that because dinosaurs had such tiny brains, they couldn't compete with the more intelligent mammals. But that idea does not seem likely to many scientists. How could the 40-ton *Apatosaurus* or the ferocious *Tyrannosaurus* be killed in a battle for his life by mammals that weighed only a few pounds?

Others have suggested that egg-eating mammals ate so many dinosaur eggs that the dinosaurs died off much faster than they were being born, and so they finally died out completely. That doesn't explain, however, why some reptiles—such as turtles, snakes, lizards, and crocodiles—did manage to survive, or why flying reptiles and marine (sea) reptiles also died out at the same time the land dinosaurs died.

Various other ideas have been suggested to explain the death of all the dinosaurs, such as disease, glandular trouble, cosmic rays from the explosion of a star (a supernova), and changes in the magnetic field of the earth. Most recently, some scientists have suggested the idea that perhaps a huge asteroid struck the earth. Supposedly this monumental collision threw three billion tons of dust into the air, blacking out the sun for several years and causing most plants to die, and so the dinosaurs died out for lack of food.

Other scientists argue strongly against this idea. If this were true, why didn't all the birds die, too? How did all the small, thin-skinned mammals manage to survive? Such a great catastrophe all over the earth would have also killed all the birds, mammals such as dogs, bears, rats, mice, and many other animals. How did such reptiles as snakes, turtles, and crocodiles survive? This scenario does not sound at all reasonable. In fact, none of the above ideas seems to explain why dinosaurs died out.

No one knows for sure why this happened. However, we believe that all of the dinosaurs may have died out after the Flood because of the many great changes that took place on the earth as a result of that flood.

In the original world, it is believed, there was once a great water vapor canopy around the earth, "The waters ... above the firmament" (Genesis 1:7). There was no rainfall on the early earth, "But a mist went up from the earth and watered the whole face of the ground" (Genesis 2:6).

The great water vapor canopy inhibited rainfall by maintaining worldwide fairly uniform mild, warm climate with none of the wide temperature changes that cause the necessary conditions for rainfall. There was no rain, and no rainbows.

The change in climate that came after the Flood could have killed many animals. We know that many of the dinosaurs lived in far northern countries, because their fossils have been found above the Arctic Circle, and in the Antarctic. Greenland, which is now covered all year long with snow and ice, at one time had a sub-tropical climate much like that of Puerto Rico. We know that because of the type of fossil animals and plants that are found on Greenland. Fossils of plants and animals that now live only in warm or mild climates are found up in the far north above the Arctic Circle, and down in the Antarctic. This means these lands, which are now frozen all or most of the year, were once as warm as Hawaii.

It was a world with no frozen Arctic or Antarctic; a world when Greenland was a near-tropic land with palm trees, and Canada was almost as warm as Florida. Lush vegetation covered much of the earth. The great plant-eating dinosaurs would have found an abundance of food. There would have been plenty of food for all the animals, and for man.

The fossils of a variety of dinosaurs have been found on the north shore of Alaska, and in Antarctica. These are places where today there are several months of darkness and it is much too cold for dinosaurs to live. But they did live there long ago! Evolutionists do not know why the earth had a worldwide warm climate in the past, but Bible-believing creationists have the answer.

What happened? What changed the climate all over the world so drastically? What could have happened to change Greenland from a beautiful, warm, green, tropical paradise into a frozen wasteland? What turned the lovely green Arctic and Antarctic areas into lands of perpetual ice? What happened to the climate of the world, and changed the lush feeding grounds of the dinosaurs in China and Utah into deserts? What caused the Ice Age?

The changes that would have occurred to the earth during and after the Flood of Noah provide the answers to many of these questions. When the dinosaurs left the Ark after the Flood, they found a world incredibly different than the one before the Flood. Food, once abundant, would have been difficult to find. Weather that had always been pleasant would now often be hostile.

The results were great changes to the earth's worldwide warm climate—from its lush green vegetation covering all the earth to the present-day situation with vast frigid areas, vast deserts, and highly changeable weather. Under these conditions, the dinosaurs failed to repopulate the earth and, consequently, died out. All we have left of these dinosaurs—great and small—which roamed the entire earth long ago, are their fossils.

Ice Age

Before the time of the Flood, it is believed there was a vast amount of water vapor in the atmosphere (it hadn't rained before the Flood). This water vapor was in a great canopy above the earth. To provide enough water for rain lasting forty days and nights, there had to be a great deal more water vapor in the atmosphere at that time than today. Today, there is only enough water vapor in the atmosphere for about one inch of rainfall (if it rained simultaneously all around the globe, the rain would last about one hour).

The Bible says that the fountains of the great deep burst open, or were broken up (meaning that the crust of the earth broke up), and the windows of heaven (or the "floodgates of the sky") were opened. Probably, as a result, the land sank down and the ocean floors came up (perhaps even large continents broke up to make smaller ones!). All of this, along with the rain, caused the whole earth to be flooded with water.

Water vapor is water in the form of an invisible gas—like that which collects on the outside of an ice-cold glass of water or on the windowpane when you blow your warm breath on it. Water vapor is transparent, not like clouds that you can see. With this vapor in the atmosphere to absorb and hold the heat from the sun, the entire earth would have been much warmer. Because of this big change in atmospheric conditions at the time of the Flood, the world became drier and cooler. What we call the Ice Age had begun.

The North and South Poles became lands of perpetual ice, and Greenland changed from a tropical paradise to a frozen wasteland. Lands that had been lush and green turned into deserts. The ocean also became cooler.

Great glaciers during the Ice Age probably covered much of Canada, the northern parts of the United States, and much of northern Europe. The North American glacier consisted of snow packed into ice, which slowly flowed out like hard taffy from a snow accumulation center in the Hudson Bay region. These glaciers sculpted grooves in rock, carved great holes that became lakes, and deposited material into layers of the earth.

In other parts of the world there was more rainfall than we have today. For example, there is evidence of ancient streams and rivers in the Sahara Desert, where rain is very infrequent today.

What caused the Ice Age? Before the Flood, the oceans were much warmer, and when the "fountains of the deep" burst forth to flood the earth, the water that spewed forth was probably very warm. Warm water evaporates more quickly. The water vapor in the air formed a "greenhouse" canopy to keep the temperatures even, but when that was gone (after the Flood), the barren lands in the northern latitudes became colder than before. The difference in temperature between the warm ocean and cold land caused intense storm patterns, and especially lots of snowfall. Volcanic eruptions caused hot debris to shield the earth from the sun's warming radiation. This also kept much of the snow from melting in the summertime. It is not known how long this Ice Age lasted after the Flood, but perhaps it was 500 to 1,000 years before the ice and snow melted enough to make the land inhabitable as it is today.

During the Ice Age, so much water was frozen that the sea level was lowered 600 feet. This helped to connect the continents. Therefore, it was not difficult for Noah and his family and the animals to go forth and multiply their kind to fill the earth, as God told them to do. When the people built the Tower of Babel and God confused their languages, the Bible records how different language groups went in different directions to start their own communities and countries.

This sudden freezing of such a large portion of the world produced many fossils of land animals. More research is being done to better understand the Ice Age and its effects on the earth.

Dinosaurs, Dragons & Beetles

Dinosaurs, Dragons and Beetles—a really dumb title? What in the world do they have to do with each other? A lot more than you'd think. Read on, you may be surprised.

Stories of dragons come from people all over the world, not from just a few isolated places. The tales come from the oldest of traditions and history. They were part of the cultures, and, in many cases, their religions.

Dr. Henry Morris writes in his book *The Genesis Record*:

> The frequent references to dragons in the Bible, as well as in the early records and traditions of most of the nations of antiquity, certainly cannot be shrugged off as mere fairy tales. Most probably they represent memories of dinosaurs handed down by tribal ancestors who encountered them before they became extinct.

It would be very hard to believe that so many people from so many different places could have come up with such similar stories and similar descriptions if such things never really existed.

According to ancient stories, dragons came in many shapes and sizes. Some could fly, some could swim, while others breathed fire.

Nebuchadnezzar had a dragon called Sirrush carved into the Ishtar Gate in Babylon. Dragons were very common subjects for statues, carvings, and paintings.

In the East (China, Japan, etc.), dragons were revered and considered to bring good luck. Dragons in Imperial China were believed to attend the births of wise emperors and philosophers. A great blue dragon was said to hover over the house where Confucius was about to be born. The bones and teeth which they thought belonged to dragons were ground up and used as medicine.

They said dragons laid eggs. (Remember, dinosaurs also laid eggs.) However, these young Chinese dragons, according to legends, were believed to incubate in the egg for 3,000 years before hatching.

In most of the rest of the world, dragons are symbols of evil and destruction.

When it comes to dragon stories, few images are as interesting as St. George and the dragon. There are many famous paintings immortalizing the dramatic moment when St. George drove his spear into the fierce but doomed dragon.

But what is the story of St. George? When did he live and what events led up to the famous event?

The story begins approximately between the years A.D. 250 and 300. It seems there was living in a great lake a terrible dragon with breath so bad it poisoned the countryside around the lake. The local people were forced to feed this beast two sheep a day to keep it content. Pretty soon they ran out of sheep and, so the story goes, began feeding it their sons and daughters. Well, they ran out of those, too. In desperation, they took the king's daughter and tied her to a stake in the field to wait for the dragon to come and eat her.

It was her lucky day because St. George just happened to be passing by. He saw the king's daughter tied up and crying, so he went to investigate. She warned him to run for his life since there was no point in both of them being eaten. Well, St. George, being a brave man, met the dragon head on and drove his lance through the dragon's evil heart. Because St. George gave the glory to Christ for the victory, the princess and then the entire population were baptized as Christians.

How much of this legend is true? We may never know how much is fact and how much is fantasy. Legends are stories about things that happened long, long before the people later telling the stories were even born. Nobody can really know, then, whether or not the stories are true, because nobody now living was there to see whether those things actually happened. Many legends, however, are believed to be about things that really did happen, although all the details in the story may not be true.

This is one of those legends that probably has a lot of truth in it. We know St. George was a real man who lived during that time period, and unfortunately we have the record of his martyrdom (put to death because of his faith) on April 23, 303.

St. George was held in the highest regard by the crusaders, and in 1350 was made patron saint of England. Great churches were named after him all over the world. We may never know the exact truth, but you can be sure he did something very special and brave.

The "dragon" in this illustration is the meat-eating Baryonyx, a dinosaur whose fossil remains were discovered in Great Briton in 1983.

Baryonyx

God has given many animals living today very specialized and effective defense capabilities that have nothing to do with teeth or claws. If the fossil skeletons of a skunk, porcupine, or an electric eel were dug up by a scientist who had never seen a living animal, would he have any idea that these animals had unique defense mechanisms?

In Job, there is a terrible animal described, called a "leviathan," that could not be stopped by swords or spears. The Bible describes a very unique defense mechanism:

> His sneezings flash forth light, and his eyes are like the eyelids of the morning. Out of his mouth go burning lights; sparks of fire shoot out. Smoke goes out of his nostrils, as from a boiling pot and burning rushes.

Job 41:18–21

Legends about fire-breathing dragons may have had more to them than you might think.

Remember the duck-billed (or hadrosaurs) dinosaurs, on pages 38 to 41, that had bony crests or inflatable sacs of skin connected to their nostrils? *Parasaurolophus* had a great bony crest with hollow chambers. Perhaps a *Parasaurolophus* could combine chemicals in his hollow crest and spray a combustible mixture, which would spontaneously ignite when contacting the oxygen in the air. Just think of how offensive a 5-ton dinosaur could be! If this sounds a little farfetched, let me tell you about a very special little beetle that is only about half an inch long.

The bombardier beetle has a marvelously complex and extremely effective defense mechanism. When threatened, he sprays a vapor, out of minature cannons in his tail, that is not only noxious but is heated to 212° F. When predatory ants, spiders, birds, frogs, or mice get a face full of this hot, irritating gas, they back off quickly and leave him alone.

The bombardier beetle has twin chambers at the rear of his body, in which he stores two chemicals—hydroquinone and hydrogen peroxide dissolved in water. If a chemist

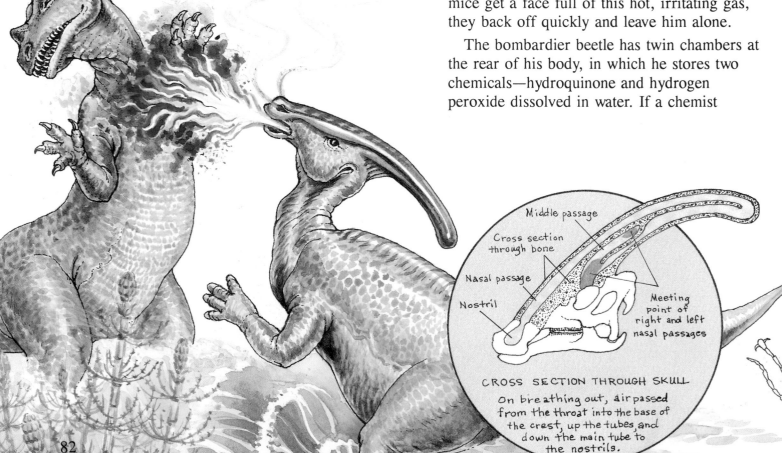

Middle passage

Cross section through bone

Nasal passage

Nostril

Meeting point of right and left nasal passages

CROSS SECTION THROUGH SKULL

On breathing out, air passed from the throat into the base of the crest, up the tubes, and down the main tube to the nostrils.

mixes these two chemicals, the hydrogen peroxide oxidizes the hydroquinone and the mixture looks like brown soup. The bombardier beetle adds a mysterious inhibitor which prevents the hydrogen peroxide from oxidizing the hydroquinone. In the beetle, this mixture of chemicals is combined with no reaction at all. The solution remains crystal clear.

When the bombardier beetle is threatened, he squirts the chemicals from the two storage chambers into two combustion tubes. In the combustion tubes, the beetle provides two enzymes—catalase and peroxidase. (An enzyme is a catalyst which makes a chemical reaction happen rapidly, without any change in the catalyst).

The chemicals and catalysts react to form another chemical, called quinone, which is very irritating. All of this happens extremely quickly in the bombardier beetle's combustion tubes, heating the liquid and gases up to 212° F, and generating a lot of pressure. When the pressure gets high enough, the bombardier beetle opens the valves on the end of his combustion tubes, and the hot gasses shoot out with great force. Scientists using special high-speed cameras have recorded both audible pops and puffs of smoke when the bombardier beetle sprays. They have also discovered that some species emit sprays in violent pulses at the rate of 500 per second.

If a tiny beetle can do something this impressive, what could an animal as large as a *Parasaurolophus* do? Those hollow crests must have been used for something. Why not a method of defense?

The little bombardier beetle is a mighty argument for creation. His defense mechanism is so complex and exacting that if it all doesn't work *exactly* right, he could explode! Evolutionists believe that he evolved from an ordinary beetle by a series of thousands of genetic mistakes (mutations). Besides the fact that all mutations are bad, the first time one of these intermediate beetles mixed the chemicals together, without the whole system in place, he'd blow up. End of beetle family line.

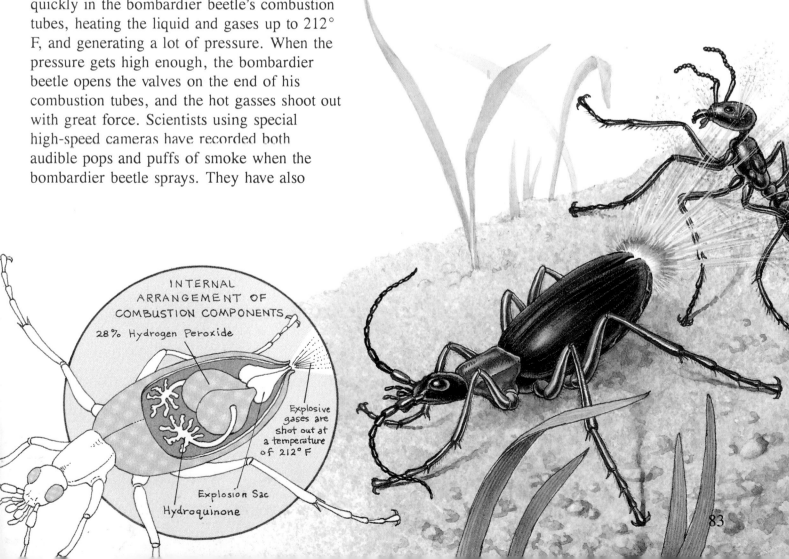

INTERNAL ARRANGEMENT OF COMBUSTION COMPONENTS

28% Hydrogen Peroxide

Explosive gases are shot out at a temperature of 212° F

Explosion Sac

Hydroquinone

Mysterious Creatures

Is all the fun and excitement of discovering new animals in the past? Is all the adventure over? **No way!** There are still unknown and uncaptured animals roaming the earth and swimming in its oceans.

In 1812, Georges Cuvier, the father of paleontology, said: "There is little hope of discovering new species of large quadrupeds." (A quadruped is an animal that walks on four feet.) Yet, only 10 years later, in 1822, Mary Mantell found the now famous *Iguanodon* tooth. As we know, there was a great deal more to discover.

There is a whole field of science called **cryptozoology**. Zoology is the study of animals and cryptozoology is the study of "hidden animals." The scientists who belong to the "International Society of Cryptozoology" investigate reports of new and

unidentified animals. Many times the investigators come up empty handed; other times the trails get pretty lively.

An exciting adventure began in England in 1860. Sir Harry Johnston, then a child, read about a strange horselike animal in Africa that had stripes but it wasn't a zebra. In 1899, he was sent to Uganda, British East Africa, as a special commissioner. He remembered the story he had read, and decided to see if he could find out more about this strange animal.

He was fortunate to have been sent to the same part of Africa where the story had originated. He had an opportunity to rescue some Wambutti pygmies from a bad situation, and he asked them about this animal. They told him it was called "okapi," and had stripes like a zebra, but only on the legs and lower part of its body. The upper part was brown and had no stripes. But the part that excited him the most was that the feet of the okapi had several toes. Since there were no known living horses that had multitoes, he wondered if this could be the long extinct three-toed horse known as *Hipparion.*

Johnston set off on an expedition to find the elusive okapi. They found tracks, but no okapi. The tracks were multitoed, just as the pygmies had said, but no animals were found no matter how long and hard they looked. His entire party became ill with malaria and had to be rescued.

In 1901, Johnston was given an okapi skin. He had a painting prepared of what he thought the animal might look like and shipped the skin and painting off to the British Museum. The director of the British Museum recognized it as a "new" animal and named it *Okapi johnstoni.* How would you like to have an animal named after you?

The first live okapi was captured in 1903. Many okapis are now prize exhibits in some of the world's zoos.

In 1939, scienctists received a real shock. A *Coelacanth* (see-la-kanth) had been caught by

Okapi

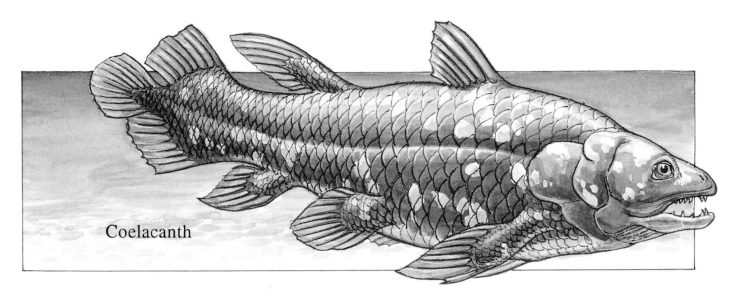

Coelacanth

fishermen off the coast of South Africa. Why was it such a shock? The coelacanth was *supposed* to have been extinct for 70 million years.

It was 14 years before a second fish came to the attention of scientists. When they investigated, they found local fishermen had been catching these fish for generations. They called it kombessa. I wonder how many other animals are known to "local" people, but unknown to science.

In November, 1976, a United States Naval research ship off the coast of Hawaii got a bit more than they expected when a parachute anchor was raised. In the net was a specimen new to science—the first specimen of a large filter-feeding shark. It was 15 feet long and had seven rows of needle-sharp teeth. The shark was dubbed "Megamouth" by the Hawaiian press, and the name stuck.

In November, 1985, a second specimen was netted off California's Santa Catalina Island. And in August, 1988, a 17-foot specimen washed up on a beach south of Perth, Western Australia. Then, two more megamouths were recorded in 1989, both in Japan's Suruga Bay.

In October, 1990, a live megamouth was found tangled in a drift swordfish net just north of San Diego. The captain of the *Moonshiner* realized he had something special—he had never seen anything like it in all his years of commercial fishing. He

Megamouth Shark

contacted scientists, who were very interested in this strange shark. The shark was carefully towed to shore, studied and photographed. The 16-foot 3-inch shark was then towed back out to sea, and released with a sonic transmitter attached.

It was found to be a vertical feeder. That is, it spends the day in deep water (several hundred feet), and ascends at night to feed. It is very possible many megamouths have been caught before, but were not recognized as anything unique.

Imagine the surprise, in 1977, on board the Japanese fishing boat *Zuiyo Maru*, near New Zealand, when a dead, very smelly "monster" came up in their net from a depth of over 900 feet. It is estimated the creature could have been dead over a month. It was 32 feet long and weighed over 4,000 pounds. The fishermen measured it, photographed it, took

tissue samples, and promptly threw it overboard before it could contaminate their "real catch."

The Japanese scientists who had flown in to see this wonderful "new" sea monster were a bit upset, to say the least. From all the evidence available to them, the scientists believed the creature to "look very much like a *Plesiosaur*" (PLEE-zee-uh-sawr). One scientist said, "It seems that these animals are not extinct after all. It is impossible for only one to have survived. There must be a group."

Several other fishing vessels were sent to try and recover the huge animal. They put their deep-water nets in and tried for several days to catch it again. Nothing! It's a wonder it was ever netted in the first place.

A strange thing happened in the North Sea—right in the middle of World War I. This report was made by German U-boat captain, Georg von Forstner:

> On 30 July 1915, our U28 torpedoed the British steamer *Iberian,* carrying a rich cargo in the North Atlantic. The steamer sank quickly, the bow sticking almost vertically into the air. When it had been gone for about twenty-five seconds, there was a violent explosion. A little later, pieces of wreckage, and among them a gigantic sea animal, writhing and struggling wildly, was shot out of the water to a height of 60 to 100 feet. At that moment I had with me in the conning tower my officer of the watch, the chief engineer, the navigator, and the helmsman. ... We did not have the time to take a photograph, for the animal sank out of sight after ten or fifteen seconds. It was about 60 feet long, was like a crocodile in shape, and had four limbs with powerful webbed feet, and a long tail tapering to a point.

The beautiful Pacific Northwest has had a number of USO (Unidentified Swimming Object) sightings. True, many USO sightings around the world are only seals, whales, rocks, logs or other well-known objects mistaken for sea monsters. Some of the encounters, however, are by very reliable people and at close range. These accounts cannot be lightly pushed aside.

One of these accounts happened in 1984 when a mechanical engineer was fishing for chinook salmon off the Spanish Banks just five miles from downtown Vancouver, Canada. Probably all he had on his mind was how good baked salmon tasted or how beautiful the ocean was.

Can you imagine his surprise when a large animal surfaced about 200 feet from him? He said it had a "whitish-tan throat, bumps like giraffe horns, large floppy ears and a somewhat pointed black snout. The shyly curious animal seemed surprised at seeing me, and intent on vacating the area. It headed rapidly out to sea, swimming very efficiently by up and down wriggling." It seems you never have a camera when you need it!

The coast from Oregon to Alaska has hundreds and hundreds of miles of islands, bays, and fjords. The waters are full of fish, and—even better for a shy sea monster—very few people. If there are "undiscovered" animals in these waters, it isn't hard to see why we know so little about them.

There are sightings all over the world every year of very large, strange animals. Many are of dead animals that have washed up on a beach. Unfortunately, they are often in an advanced state of decay and scientists can only make a guess as to what they might be.

Many sightings of "sea monsters" seem to fit descriptions of *Plesiosaurus* or *Mosasaurus*. **Mosasaurus** (mo-zuh-SAWR-us) was a giant marine lizard that grew to 50 feet or more. It was a meat-eater that swam close to the surface of oceans all over the world.

Did you know that over 70 percent of the earth's surface is covered by water? Or that the average depth of the oceans is over two miles? If we don't even know all of the animals on land, just think of what might be underwater.

Is the search for "new" animals over? What do you think? Who knows what adventures are waiting for YOU!

Index

Pages in bold have illustrations.